Conversations with God

book 4

Also by Neale Donald Walsch

Conversations with God

book 4
• Awaken the Species •

A New and Unexpected Dialogue

Neale Donald Walsch

RAINBOW RIDGE
BOOKS

Cover and interior design by Frame25 Productions
Cover photo © Tithi Luadthong c/o Shutterstock.com

Published by:
Rainbow Ridge Books, LLC
140 Rainbow Ridge Road
Faber, Virginia 22938
www.rainbowridgebooks.com
434-361-1723

If you are unable to order this book from your local
bookseller, you may order directly from the distributor.

Square One Publishers, Inc.
115 Herricks Road
Garden City Park, NY 11040
Phone: (516) 535-2010
Fax: (516) 535-2014
Toll-free: 877-900-BOOK

Visit the author at:
www.CWGConnect.com

Library of Congress Cataloging-in-Publication Data applied for.

ISBN 978-1-937907-49-5

10 9 8 7 6 5 4 3 2 1

Printed on acid-free recycled
paper in Canada

To those who see that neither
their Life nor their world
is as wonderful as it was meant to be,
but who know that both *can* be,
and who now choose to make it so.

Author's Note

I am aware that in the most recent book in the *Conversations with God* series—*Home with God in a Life That Never Ends,* written and published ten years prior to this writing—it was indicated that it would be the final of these dialogues to be published and widely distributed by me. Yet life is an ever-changing mosaic, and given that all of us are One with God, we do have the ability to create what filmmakers would call an "alternate ending" to any story. Apparently, this is what has happened here. A new decision appears to have been made at a Superconscious level (the level at which all souls function).

I could have kept this latest dialogue private, but everything within me shouted, "Don't you dare." With this public distribution of a new word-for-word transcription of my most recent conversation with God, I feel that I am keeping a promise to God to do whatever I might be able to do to continue to place into the world the most important information I have ever been given—information that, it has been demonstrated to me, can change in a positive way the daily experience of millions of people around the world.

Notwithstanding the fact that all of the world's major religions speak of divine revelation from God to humans as having occurred throughout history, I perfectly well understand it if some people feel that such a blessed event would presumably not occur in the life of an utterly imperfect and fault-ridden person such as myself. I have always said, however, that it is not me, in the singular, who has conversations with God, but all of us, in the plural, all the time. Most people are simply calling it something else.

All of us have the ability to access the source of highest wisdom within us—which we are invited to consider to be God working in and through us. The dialogue itself puts this succinctly, in the voice of The Divine: "I talk to everyone all the time. The question is not, *To whom do I talk?* The question is, *Who listens?"*

I therefore invite you to set aside whatever natural skepticism may arise regarding the source of the information found here, and to focus instead on whether or not what has been offered in this process has any value in the living of your individual life and, more broadly, in the understanding of Life Itself.

This text contains much information about life and death—and the time in between. It is filled with probably more metaphysical data than you may have been exposed to in one place in a very long time. At one point in the dialogue that follows you may find yourself saying, "Speculation or fact, this is utterly fascinating," yet then fairly be asking, "but what good is knowing all of this? What does it have to do with my life, and the improving of it—much less the improving of the lives of all of us on Earth?"

You will see here that I asked question after question in my own effort to render this dialogue meaningful and relevant. What I know is that today, with everything that's going on in the world, people are yearning and searching for a message of hope, faith, healing, and change. I found that this latest conversation with God offered me that, and this is why I let myself publicly share it. The exchange here contains a few tough assessments of where we are today, yet these are offered not as judgments, but as flashlights, illuminating what we are now being invited to see and empowered to do.

I know it sounds trite, but a Better Tomorrow for us as individuals and for our civilization is possible. Very, *very* possible, if we will choose it. As the dialogue here makes clear, we are but One Decision away. I hope you'll decide to make that decision after reading what follows.

Introduction

I awoke from a sound sleep on August 2, 2016. It was The Urge that awakened me. I knew it well. I hadn't felt it in nearly 10 years, but I knew it well.

I had no idea what time it was, but I thought to myself, "If it's 4:23, will I need more of a sign than that?"

I glanced at the clock on my bedside table.

4:13 a.m.

Of course. Just enough time to pull myself out of bed for my 4:23 "appointment."

The first dialogue I ever had with God began at 4:23 in the morning. And every morning for weeks I would be awakened between 4:15 and 4:30 by a deep inward urge: *Get back to the dialogue.*

This pattern continued for months (and subsequently, for years). I wondered if there was any significance to the timing of it, but ultimately released any need to know.

When the first conversations with God material, scribbled on yellow legal pads, actually became a published book (I was told in the dialogue that it would, so I sent it to a publisher on a dare), I thought that maybe something important had taken place here. And when over a million people obtained the book, and I saw it being translated into 37 languages, I was shocked into certainty about that.

Then it came to pass that requests for me to speak outside the U.S. began arriving, and I had to find my birth certificate in order to apply for a passport. It was nowhere to be found among my personal papers, so I applied to the records department of the government where I was born, paying the fee and asking to be sent an official copy.

I was stunned when I opened the envelope and examined the document.

TIME OF BIRTH: 4:23 A.M.

Of course.

The fact that this experience of Divine connection always seemed to be initiated near the time every day that I came into this world somehow seemed meaningful to me. At the very least, I could not ignore the perfect symmetry of it.

Through the years, then, whenever I found myself suddenly wide awake between 4:15 and 4:30 in the morning, eyes staring at the ceiling, a certain energy coursing through my body, I knew what was going on. I got up immediately, raced to my laptop, and opened myself to whatever wanted to come through.

And so it was on this day, August 2, 2016. I've just thrown back the covers and pulled myself out of bed. Now here I am at the keyboard. The only thing is, I didn't think I'd be doing this again.

Let me explain.

All of us are having what I have come to call conversations with God all the time. This was made clear to me on page five of the over 3,000 pages of the published CWG dialogues. So my experience was not unique, not uncommon. What *was* perhaps a bit unusual was that I made a written record of my innermost encounters, and then sent it to a publisher—who in turn *actually printed it* and placed it in bookstores.

I have come to understand and to experience that I (and all of us) have a deep and personal connection with God all the time, and that we may have an actual communication with The Divine, asking for guidance, help, insight, and assistance, whenever we wish. That was, in fact, *the point of the book.* It was placed into the world to open other people everywhere to this experience; to invite them to a new and more personal relationship with God.

The feeling that I *must* have such a dialogue, however—that "the time has come" for such an interaction, signaled by a deep inner feeling welling within me that cannot be ignored—is something else altogether. I experience this as a feeling that *comes over me,* and I haven't had this feeling for nearly ten years. So I've held the idea that I had encountered it for the last time.

Oh, I knew I'd be writing again. I'll always be writing something. A column for *Huffington Post.* A blog for CWG Connect. A Facebook entry. An answer to someone posting a question at Ask Neale. Even a full-length book exploring in depth the messages I've received. Something.

But another on-paper conversation with God? Another back-and-forth dialogue with Deity? I thought those days were over. I thought that process was complete.

I was wrong.

1

I didn't think I'd ever be doing this again. I thought this process was complete.

> There is more to do. One more invitation, Dear One.

I've already accepted two: Change the world's mind about God, and give people back to themselves. I thought that was it.

> I know. It wasn't time yet for the third.

Now it is?

> Now it is.

Okay, what's the third? And will this be the last invitation?

> Yes, this will be the last. And these invitations are, by the way, not just for you. They're for everyone—although not everyone will accept them.
> Those who will accept them will self-identify.

I've always understood that the messages were not just for me. About those first two invitations, I've always understood that.

> So now comes the third and final invitation. Because it's The Perfect Time for Advancement on your planet.

That sounds really exciting, especially when it feels like just the opposite. It seems as though our civilization is moving backward. It feels like we're becoming less civil, less tolerant, less capable of controlling our indulgences (to say nothing of our anger), less able to access the better angels of our nature.

> I'm glad that you're seeing this, experiencing this, because if you pay attention to what's happening with you and around you—and do what you feel inwardly called to do in response to it—there's nothing to worry about.

Well, it looks bad to me, but I don't know if I'm getting into my own judgment about things and can't see clearly. I mean, there's a lot going on around this planet that I think shouldn't be happening.

> It's not about what "should" or "should not" be happening. It's about what *is* happening—both in your individual and highly personal experience, as well as the experience of the collective called humanity—and how you can change, actually

rather dramatically, what you may feel are the worst parts of that.

This is The Perfect Time for you to begin making those alterations, because what's happening now—environmentally, politically, economically, socially, and spiritually—is providing you with conspicuous and unmistakable, incontrovertible and crystal clear signs on how you can do that.

And so it's time for the Third Invitation.

Okay, I'm ready. We're all ready. What is it? What's the Third Invitation?

Awaken the species.

2

Well, *that's* not too ambitious.

Is there anything too ambitious for God?

I meant for *me.*

So did I.

I see what you mean.

Do you? Or have you forgotten Who You Are . . . ?

No. Well, *yes* . . . in the sense that I don't act that way. I mean, I understand intellectually that God resides within me, that I am an Individuation of Divinity, I just don't experience it functionally.

You may wish to begin.

That's easier said than done.

As long as you keep saying that, you'll find it to be true. Yet you can't awaken the species until you awaken yourself.

I know, I know . . . I'm trying as hard as I can.

> You may want to try harder. It's The Perfect Time
> for Advancement.

You're making that point.

> Will you try harder then? All of you?

I can't speak for anyone else, but I'm in. Tell me how I can awaken more quickly. There's not a person on Earth who doesn't want to know how to do that.

> The fastest way to awaken more quickly is to be
> the cause of someone else awakening more quickly.

But how can I "be the cause" of someone *else* awakening if I'm not awake?

> This is interesting. This is what is called a Divine
> Dichotomy—when two apparently contradictory
> truths exist simultaneously in the same space.
> The truth is that you *are* awake, you just don't
> know that you are. So in that sense, you're not.
> You're not awake to the fact that you're awake.
> So it feels as if you're *not* awake.

Can you help me with that? I felt like we just went around in circles there.

Have you ever heard a noise in the middle of the night and thought it was part of a dream, only to be surprised to find that you're actually awake?

Sure. That's happened to all of us.

There you are.

Okay, so let's agree that I'm awake, but just don't know it yet. What could make me *realize* that I'm awake?

Have you ever been *scared* awake by a nightmare?

Yes, again. We've all had that experience as well.

You're being scared awake right now, by some of the conditions on your planet, some of which have become nightmarish.

You said yourself it feels like you're going backward.

In my own life sometimes, not just globally.

Observing this is very good. It will cause you to know that you're awake, and that this is not just a bad dream, it's a reality that you no longer choose.

You're becoming more and more conscious every day of what's going on, and that's going to help you remember Who You Are—and motivate you to begin acting like it.

That's all that has to happen here. That's all that's going to be required for all of you who already feel that you are awake to bring an end to every nightmarish condition. You simply need to *awaken* to the fact that you're already awake, and that there's something you can do about what you see happening all around you.

I'm not sure I'm up to trying to save the world.

This is not about saving the world. This is about your personal spiritual journey; it is about your individual evolution. It can be the most exciting, enthralling time you've experienced since your birth.

And the world may indeed change, may indeed be "saved," by your decision to begin acting as Who You Really Are—but that will not have been the point of it.

It is your personal evolution that will be the point and the purpose of every and any change you make in how you move through, and experience, the world.

If it is your desire to demonstrate Who You Really Are—and one way you see yourself doing it is by assisting in ending the suffering of others, bringing healing to a planet, and affecting in a positive way the future of those you love—then you will not feel burdened by an "assignment too big," but rather, joyously thrilled about the opportunity Life has placed before you in this Perfect Time to Advance.

The Third Invitation is to awaken, as part of your process of personal evolution, the many members of your species who are already awake, to the *fact* that they are, and then to inspire them to begin acting like it also, so to model and inspire an awakened behavior for those others who are still asleep—and to do this all because this is what your personal evolution calls you to.

Thank you. I "get it." But there is this lingering question. If many people are already awake, why *aren't* they acting like it? Are you telling me that not one of them—not a single one—*knows* they are awake? They're all still thinking they're just "dreaming" what sometimes feels like a nightmare called "today's news" on Earth?

No. Many of them know that what's happening is real, and they are awake to who they are and what it would take for them to awaken the rest of the species.

Okay, then my question still lingers. If there are so many humans who know they are awake, why is the world the way it is? I'm a perfect example. Every day I do something or say something or think something that does not in any way resemble the behavior of someone who is "awakened." If I know that I am awake, as you claim, then why do I behave the way I do?

Because being awake and knowing what you know . . . and having all that you know fully integrated into your life . . . are two different things.

Sometimes—particularly when you're very young or acting immaturely—it's more attractive to you to pretend that you don't know what you know. Or just to ignore the fact that you know.

And sometimes, you simply forget.

Did your father ever say to you, "Why would you do such a thing *when you know better?*"

Of course. I heard that a hundred times.

Make it a hundred and one.

Look, yours is a very young species. You are like children. You are the toddlers of the universe. So you go around doing things that you know are not good for you, because it seems like more fun in the moment. Or you simply forget what you've been told.

This is the story of your species' collective experience on Earth. You've let it be *your* experience as an individual, too, *even though you know better*.

You're not just observing non-beneficial behaviors in others, you're actually engaging in such behaviors yourself.

But now it will be beneficial for you to set aside your childish behaviors.

I know.

And I know that you know. That's what I've been saying here.

Even those who did *not* know before, know now. It's becoming too obvious for even the most immature members of your emerging species to not see it, to not realize it, or to pretend they don't know.

Yet you're still not *acting* as if you know. You're not integrating what you know. So you know, but you're not acting as if you *know* that you know.

9

You're awake to Who You Are and to What Is True, but your behavior does not reflect this. You continue to act as if you're sleepwalking.

Now if you don't want to walk into a wall or off a cliff, you would do well to wake up to the fact that you're already awake, that you're not dreaming about some of the nightmarish conditions on Earth. And that you're not "making it up" or imagining that this very day is The Perfect Time to Advance in your evolution.

I got it! You keep saying it and I got it. I understand. And I'm going to bet that others reading this now understand, too. This is good news for everyone.

It is. And I *am* being emphatic. I *am* repeating myself.

This whole dialogue that you've felt called to have is about repeating other things I've said to you in other conversations.

It's about you hearing it again, and now getting *all of it*. It's about putting everything together as you move toward Full Integration, then feeling free to accept The Third Invitation.

Feel free to awaken your species, because this really is The Perfect Time to Advance.

3

Why do you care so much? I thought God doesn't take a position one way or the other on temporal matters.

Are you saying that you have a preference here, that you're deeply concerned about how my life, and everything else in life on Earth, turns out? And if you really are the God of this universe, and you do have a preference, how can you not get what you want?

I hope these are fair questions, because some people are going to be confused.

Every question is a fair question. Your opportunity (and the opportunity of everyone who self-identifies as one who sees helping others on their evolutionary path as part of *their* evolutionary journey) is to do what you can do to awaken your species, primarily by your behavior. For it is what you do, it is how you *are* in the world, that will shake people awake, that will startle them into seeing what their own possibilities are.

Of lesser importance, but also of value, will be what you say to others; having the courage to share not widely accepted words and thoughts and ideas that might serve to open a road to greater clarity for many people.

Now, to answer the present question: I do not "want" you to awaken your species, any more than I "want" anything at all. Please be clear. God lives in "want" of nothing. Anything God wants, God can have.

Yet God does have desires. It is God's desire that fuels the engine of creation. It is Divine Desire that powers the universe.

Okay, we'll use the word "desire" then. If God "desires" humanity to awaken—and I presume this is to preserve and improve its way of life—is there any question that this is going to happen?

God's desire is not that particular outcomes occur, but that the sentient beings in God's universe be fully empowered to create what they want.

If all the sentient beings of the universe had no choice but to do exactly what God orders them to do, you would live in a universe populated by machines. Automatons. Robots. Androids.

This would defeat the whole purpose of God having created sentient beings in the first place— which is to allow God to experience Itself as what It is: The Free Will Creator of Its Own Experience.

It is critical to understand that God is both The Creator and The Created. There is no separation between the two.

I know this. I am very clear that there is nothing that is *not* God.

That's exactly what is true.

God experiences the act of "creation," therefore, not by requiring all of Itself to follow orders, but in exactly the opposite way: by allowing and empowering all of Its creations to create whatever they wish.

In this the Parts of God demonstrate the fundamental characteristic of The Whole:

Freedom.

Absolute freedom to create as only a Pure Creator could, without limitation or restriction of any kind.

This is the power given to all sentient beings. It is the power given to humans.

So do you now understand? My desire is not that humanity be fully awakened. My desire is that *you* always be empowered to have and to create, to express and to experience, whatever you wish. If that means being awakened, wonderful. If that means not awakening, fine. I have no preference in the matter, except that your preference be fulfilled.

Then why is the Third Invitation extended by *you?* This is not us coming to you, this feels like *you* coming to *us.*

But you *are* coming to me. You've asked me, you've *all* asked me, for help. Everything that you think and say and pray for tells me that you want your life to change. And that you want life on Earth to be different.

Do you imagine that I don't hear this?

What is clear is that the only way your own life, and the life of your species, is *going* to change for the better is by awakening. And so, awakening becomes the agenda.

Yet this is *your* agenda, *your* prayer, this is what *you* want. My role is simply to empower you to create what you wish.

That is why I've extended to you the Third Invitation.

Sorry, but it still feels as if an "invitation" is *you* reaching out to *us*.

I'm going to answer that. But first, answer this for me, because others following this conversation may be wondering: Why is all of this so important to you? Why are you spending so much time on "who asked who?"

Because if all of this *is* you coming to *us*, it could feel to some very much like a command, not an opportunity; like an order, not an invitation. I know that you do not issue "orders" or give us "commandments," but this invitation of yours could seem to some like one of those mobster movies, when Don Corleone says: "I'm going to make him an offer he can't refuse."

Not that I'm comparing you to a mobster, but . . . I mean . . . who says *no* to God?

Plenty of people, actually.

Okay, I shouldn't have asked . . . but the real question is: Is this an "order" from God? Are we being commanded here?

No. As you've pointed out, I do not "command" anything or anyone. I have no need to.

Think of it this way. If a friend or loved one knocks on your front door, have *you* gone to *them*, or have they come to you?

They've come to me, of course.

And if you open the door and invite them in, is your invitation a *command*, or a loving response to their having knocked on your door?

Nice. Nice analogy. So you're saying we've knocked on your door.

My dear, you're practically breaking it down. You, and half the human race.

Can you not hear the loudest call of your species?

"Help us! Somebody, please, help us change."

Yes, I can hear it. Arising from within my own heart, I hear it.

And so I have extended the Third Invitation.

There are still those who will say: You're the God here, not us. Instead of inviting *humans* to awaken their species, why don't *you* just do it?

Then repeat to them, over and over again: God's function is to empower *you* to make happen what you wish to make happen, not to make it happen *for* you.

My role is to give you the freedom and the means to create your own reality, produce your own future, generate your own outcome.

The point is to keep *you* in the role of Creator.

I never intended for humans to be simply assembly line workers, putting together what I have designed. My intention from the beginning was to put you at the drafting board, coming up with your *own* design.

Then *you* are on the assembly line, putting together what *we* have designed!

My turn to say, "Nice analogy."

The assembly line provides the means by which the designer turns ideas into reality. There are some constraints, however, in this case. I will not assemble the parts to blow up the whole factory.

We're speaking metaphorically here, of course.

So we can end our way of life here on Earth . . .

. . . if that's what you choose . . .

. . . but we can't "disassemble" the "assembly line." We can affect our local reality, but we can't affect Ultimate Reality.

That's correct. You've got it. You understand.

So, sticking with your metaphor, you're inviting us to not set fire to our own drafting table.

> Exactly. And to notice that, right now, some of you—a small percentage of you, but enough of you to be dangerous to yourselves—are behaving like children playing with matches.

Uh-oh.

> Yes. But that's what makes this The Perfect Time for Advancement.

Because we're starting to feel the heat?

> Nice metaphor.
> So . . . to stick with it . . . yes, you're feeling the heat and you can still take those matches out of their hands.

4

I know it may not seem like it from our actions, but humans really do want to survive. That's why we're crying for help. Most humans say that "survival" is the basic instinct.

Actually, survival is not your basic instinct. If you all followed your basic instinct, the survival of your species would not be in question. It would be guaranteed.

I know.

The basic instinct of humanity is the expression of every human's True Identity—which is Divinity.

In human terms, this translates to Pure Love. Love that knows no condition and expresses itself at any cost.

That is the fundamental impulse, which is why humans run *into* a burning building, rather than away from it, if they hear a baby crying.

At the highest level, at the instant when the most urgent decision must be made, most people don't stand there weighing the odds of their survival while the baby is crying. They do what it is in their True Nature to do.

In moments such as this you understand that there is no way you can cease to exist. The spirit of you, the essence of Who You Are, will live forever and ever—and at the deepest place within, you are clear about this. Survival, therefore, ceases to be the issue. It is not a question of *whether* you will live, but *how* you will live—whether it's for another twenty years or another twenty minutes.

Now it's true that you may have a strong desire to continue living in your present physical form for more than twenty more minutes, but your basic instinct to express Divinity by becoming the personification of unconditional love outweighs and overrides this desire.

Sadly, not every member of your species experiences this level of clarity during life's ordinary moments. The number who do, in fact, is very low.

It is easy to get lost in the labyrinth of life. It's only at the most critical times, when "the chips are down," that most humans act as if they are "out of their mind"—because they *are*, quite literally. They are following, instead, the impulse of their soul.

If humans followed the impulse of their soul in *every* moment, they would create Heaven on Earth overnight. They could do this by simply seeing every minute of every day as a Burning Building Moment. A moment when we do, in fact, easily and instantly access the better angels of our nature.

This is what all those who have self-identified as choosing to assist in the awakening of your species are going to be doing. They will be following the impulse of their soul in every moment, and they will be encouraging others to do so, even as they seek to model how it is done.

But remember that yours is a very young species, and so not many of you understand why you are on Earth, nor embrace the implications of your everlasting Life with God.

If humans imagine there to be any kind of everlasting life at all, most believe it to be some form of eternal *reward or punishment*, viewing the Kingdom of God as a meritocracy. Thus, they have created a reward or punishment world, reflecting in physical reality an utterly inaccurate understanding of Ultimate Reality.

Yes, yes, I know. We've talked about these false notions before, in previous exchanges.

Now let's get back to the point made earlier, which is that most of you would like your species to continue to exist in its present physical form.

You want your children and your children's children to have the same opportunity you have had—the opportunity to experience this wonderful physical planet, this special and beautiful environment, and this particular expression of life.

Yet here is the irony. Even as you tell yourself that you want your species to continue and to improve its way of life, many of you do things that are making it very difficult.

Not on *purpose.*

> No. Not on purpose. But that's the point. Your species is not "on purpose" in the matter of how you are living your collective lives. Many of you say one thing and do another.
> And this is the most important matter facing the human race if you *truly* want to take advantage of this being The Perfect Time for Advancement within your species, allowing it to continue to exist in a wonderful and pleasant version of physicality.

And we're asking for a little help here right now, because our "version of physicality" is not so wonderful and not so pleasant for too many members of our species.

Most of the systems we've put into place to create a better life for all of us on this planet have not produced those results.

Our political systems, for instance, have produced continual disagreement and disarray. Our economic systems have produced increasing poverty and massive economic inequality. Our health care systems are not doing nearly enough to eliminate inequality of access to modern medicines and health care services. Our social systems more and more generate discordance and disparity, to say nothing of frequent injustice.

And, saddest of all, our spiritual systems have in too many ways and too many places produced bitter righteousness, shocking intolerance, widespread anger, deep-seated hatred, and self-justified violence.

Do you see what I mean when I say that you are already awake? You're observing things clearly here. There are exceptions, of course, but the accuracy of your overall assessment is everywhere in evidence.

5

I don't want to point to nothing but "what's wrong," though. I want to talk about how easy it can be for us to change things with one simple up-shift in our collective consciousness.

It *will* be easy. Remarkably easy.

Yet you can't "change things" unless you know what it is you want to change. So some discussion of what's not going well can be very useful, allowing humanity to know where it may wish to make some improvements.

This is especially true with people who hold a "see no evil, hear no evil, speak no evil" mentality, and don't normally look at these kinds of things.

Yes. But I can see apologists lining up right now to say, "Wait just a minute! We've made huge progress!" They will say we have to look at how far humanity has advanced. And they will be accurate in asserting that things are not as bad as they used to be.

So what would you say to them?

I would say, "Yes, but *is that it?* Is that the most we can say about our global experience? *"Things are not as bad as they used to be!"* Can we not at least also say that our species has finally become *civilized?*

Then I would invite them to be the judge. And I'd point out things that not many people know—or think about. Or *want* to think about.

Such as?

Such as the fact that more than 1.5 billion people in this very moment do not have electricity in this, the 21st century. Such as the fact that a *higher* number, over 1.6 billion, do not even have access to clean water. Such as the fact that a much higher number still, over 2.5 billion, do not have toilets.

Now some of this may seem like simply inconveniences, but these conditions have enormous implications. More than 19,000 children die each *day* on this planet from preventable health issues, such as malaria, diarrhea and pneumonia.

And then there is this problem—which we could solve virtually overnight if we really wanted to: over 650 children die on this planet every hour of starvation.

In the meantime, 85 of the world's richest people hold more wealth than 3.5 billion . . . that's half the planet's population . . . *combined.*

Many people insist that there's nothing wrong with this, and that this final statistic has nothing to do with the earlier ones.

"So," I would say to those apologists, "What do you think? Is this a civilized species?"

And what do you think their response would be?

Well, I've actually had this kind of discussion, and many people become defensive. Especially if they're among the smallest percentage of the world's population holding or controlling the largest percentage of its wealth and resources.

They say that those who "have" are doing their best to get more to those who "have not." And many of them, if not most of them, *have* done their best. It's not the individuals who are the problem, it's the institutions of society. It's how the "system" is set up. It's the economic structures and constructions.

Yours is a young species, still trying to find its way.

The result is that there are many who describe our species as "civilized" in spite of the fact that we're still building, and actually threatening the use of, weapons of mass destruction in a global community that has found it impossible to create a way to simply get along. And I keep wondering: Is this civilized?

There are many who describe our species as "civilized" in spite of the fact that we're still killing human beings intentionally as a means of teaching human beings that killing humans beings intentionally is not okay—and we fail to see the contradiction. And I keep wondering: Does this make sense?

There are many who describe our species as "civilized" in spite of the fact that we're still claiming that a loving God does not want people who cherish each other to marry each other if they are the same sex as each other—

or even if they are *not* the same sex, but are of different races, religions, tribes, or cultures. And I keep wondering: Is this our definition of love?

There are many who describe our species as "civilized" in spite of the fact that we're still brutally killing and eating the flesh of other living creatures, pretending that those creatures are not sufficiently self-aware to experience "suffering" in the way that they are raised and how they are slaughtered—or that it doesn't matter even if they do experience suffering, because humans have *domination* over them and get to do with them as we want, how we want, when we want. And I keep wondering: Is this how we define the human species as humane?

There are many who describe our species as "civilized" in spite of the fact that we're still smoking and ingesting known carcinogens, ignoring how huge numbers of us are suffering from what we are doing *to ourselves,* and that we're still abusing alcohol and drugs, pretending that these are substances we can handle—all the while we're not handling them at all, but seeing these things alter our very personality, the root of our *being*. And I keep wondering: Is this a measure of our intelligence?

These conditions presenting themselves in such an unavoidably visible, dramatically obvious way are what make this The Perfect Time for Advancement.

Fifty years ago—even twenty years ago—before the vast expansion of the Internet and the explosively global reach of social media, those conditions existed with far fewer people noticing them.

I see what you're saying. The "time is right" for humanity to really be able to do something about all this now, because now everybody can know, *everyone*—not just a few people here and there in activist organizations, academic institutions, or government offices—can be aware of what the problems are, and how *widespread* they are.

Can you imagine 1.6 billion people not even having access to clean water, in the first quarter of the 21st century, on a planet whose inhabitants consider themselves to be evolved?

> So you're seeing that you can't solve problems you don't know about—and that knowing about them and talking more and more about them is something you can celebrate, because it creates the perfect climate within which conditions are finally addressed and solutions can be created.

Exactly! Or to put this another way, necessity is the mother of invention.

I have enormous hope that the human venture will become one of the most successful and joyous expressions of life in the cosmos. I'm clear that we are but One Decision Away from creating this.

> And what is this One Decision?

6

I believe that we can change the global experience of our entire species by making the decision to open-mindedly, genuinely, and unrestrictedly explore—then open-heartedly, joyously, and unreservedly accept—the reality of Who We Really Are.

Wonderfully put.

And this will be an enormously impactful decision as it relates to your individual evolutionary process.

Remember, what we're discussing here is not just changing world conditions, but changing the conditions in everyone's personal life, in everyone's day-to-day experience. In fact, as noted before, this is where everything starts. This is where it begins.

The Third Invitation is about how one's individual life is going, the way it is feeling, and what it is presenting as its next manifestation.

You can be a transformed Self if you accept the invitation to awaken the species, because it is just as I said at the outset: The fastest way to awaken the Self is to awaken another.

When you start focusing on this, you will realize that you already *are* awake—and this will make all the difference.

It will change the way you think, the way you speak, the way you act, and the way you choose to *be* in every moment and situation.

That, in turn, will affect both what is drawn *to* you in your life, and how you experience what*ever* comes your way.

Now the only question is whether humanity will make that One Decision. But I believe it *can be done*. It's not a pipe dream, completely out of reach and utterly out of the question.

It absolutely is not. It is, though, going to invite and require a wonderful shift in individual and group consciousness. A quantum expansion of humanity's perspective and perception. A towering and joyful rise in awareness.

But, to re-emphasize, it is possible, or you would not be saying that this is The Perfect Time for Advancement.

Not only is it possible, it is happening now. You wouldn't be having this conversation—and no one would be following it—if such a shift in consciousness wasn't right now evident and occurring.

The next step is for more and more humans to awaken.

I understand the Third Invitation. I totally get it now. And so does everyone else who's tracking this. I suspect there will be many people self-selecting to move their own personal evolution forward by humbly lending their energies to the awakening of the species in whatever small way they can through working on their own awakening.

> And to help all of you accomplish this, you are invited to turn to Higher Aspects of the One Reality of which you are an integral part.

Wait. Hold it. I was just totally "getting" everything you've said here, and now you've lost me.

> You are encouraged to notice that you not alone as you face the challenges now confronting your species.

Yes, I know that nearly everybody on Earth is concerned about this. There aren't many people on this planet who aren't worried about the future, and trying, each in their own way, to do something about creating a better tomorrow.

The challenge here is that we've tried so many things, and we haven't yet found the answer. We haven't yet, as I've said, found a way to simply get along. We can't even find a way to stop killing each other.

> So maybe it's time to get help from those who *have* found a way.

As I just said, practically everybody on Earth has tried and so far failed.

> Then turn to those who are not on Earth.

I'm sorry . . . ?

Perhaps it's time to get help from those who are not on Earth, who know all about life on Earth, but are not *from* Earth.

7

Whoa. What kind of door have you just opened here?

A door that has always been open. You simply haven't walked through it yet.

Are we talking beings from outer space?

Do you think there are such beings?

Well, yes, I do. You even told me there were. We had a long discussion about them from Chapter 16 to the end of *Conversations with God, Book 3*.

And what did I say there?

You said that there were many advanced civilizations in the universe. Not dozens, not hundreds, but *thousands*. You spoke extensively about what you called "Highly Evolved Beings," for which we created the acronym "HEBs." And you described most of the underpinnings of life in highly evolved societies.

Remember that you said this, because it's going to play a role in where we go later in *this* dialogue.

Okay, I will. And what I wanted to say now is that none of what was shared previously about advanced civilizations elsewhere seemed outside the realm of possibility to me. None of it seemed far-fetched. We're in, after all, a huge universe. What *does* seem far-fetched is the idea that *we* are the only sentient beings in it. The chances of *that* must be one-in-a-centillion.

Actually, there's no chance of that at all. Of *course* there are other sentient beings in the universe. They're all over the place.

And these beings are ready to help us? Is that what you're saying now?

I'm saying that you need not think that you are alone in accepting the invitation to awaken your species.

Well, we don't. You said yourself that we've turned to *you*. We've knocked on your door. We've turned to God. Shouldn't that be enough? We turn to God and you tell us to turn to *other life forms in the universe?*

Divinity comes in many shapes. The form that *you* take is one of them. So if you want to experience that God is helping you, look to yourselves and your own highest wisdom—but then don't hesitate to look as well to all of the Manifestations of Divinity available to assist you.

Don't look right past, or right through, those who may be opening the door in response to your knock.

You really are talking about beings from off this planet, aren't you?

> I am.

I'm sure that many humans may think that our help will come from the heavens, but not from *other life forms in* the heavens!

> It would be short-sighted to ignore or deny that possibility.

So let me get this straight, because I don't want there to be any confusion here. You're saying that other life forms in the universe are choosing to help us?

> Some, yes. Not all other life forms, but some.
> Not all other life forms are benevolent.

Well, *that's* a bit scary.

> Why? Even *humans* are not all benevolent. Many of you are not even helping yourselves. And you're actually hurting each other.

Yes, but we're a very young species. And we've agreed that many humans are acting like children. You've said that many of the other species of sentient beings in the universe are far more advanced than we are.

> That does not mean that they would in every case be helpful to you. Some of them are violent.

Advanced life forms from elsewhere in the universe are violent?

Some of them, yes.

If they are so "advanced," how can they still be violent?

There's a difference between being highly advanced and being highly evolved.

If people from 2,000 years ago could leapfrog time and appear on your planet right now, do you think they would say that today's inhabitants of Earth are "advanced"?

I imagine that they would, yes.

And yet, are today's inhabitants of the Earth not violent?

Yes. Sadly, yes, we are.

So technological advancement does not necessarily mean advancement morally, ethically, consciously, or spiritually—is that what you're saying?

Point made.

Do not assume, then, that all other life forms in the universe have chosen to be of help as you seek to awaken humanity. Advanced civilizations do not automatically equate to highly evolved civilizations.

Would we even be able to know the difference? For that matter, are we even able to know that there *are* Highly Evolved Beings choosing to help us? I mean, you're saying that here, but is it possible for those of us on Earth to know this *in our experience* without freaking out?

And even more important, *how* are these Highly Evolved Beings helping us? By hovering around us—literally or metaphorically—and watching over us to make sure we don't hurt ourselves too badly? By actually visiting us, and working with us in a physical way right here on Earth? By planting ideas in our heads from afar?

> Good. Keep going. These are not unimportant questions.

And the answers?

> The answer to all of the above is yes.

Um . . . okaaay. I need you to elaborate. Would you care to expand on that?

> We'll have to take your questions one at a time.

Whatever works.

> You will know the difference between other life forms who are helpful and may not be helpful by feeling the vibration.

Wow, what a "New Age" answer. Excuse me . . . I mean, I'm sorry . . . but I can already hear tons of people saying, "What a sappy New Age answer. *Feel the vibe*, man."

Have you ever walked into a room, a bar, or a restaurant and decided within seconds that you didn't want to be there, turned right around and walked back out?

Have you ever put on a shirt or a blouse as you dressed to go somewhere, then took it off immediately, knowing that it was not the right one?

Have you ever met a person and felt an inner awareness that you really are not supposed to have much to do with them? Or, looked at from the other side, have you ever experienced "love at first sight"?

Sure. Most of us have had at least one of those experiences.

And did you think of them as "sappy, New Age" experiences—or just part of life?

Thanks, I got it. So if we can feel the vibration of restaurants, blouses, and people, we can feel the vibration of other life forms—and we would know immediately which ones feel good to us, and helpful, and which ones do not.

Yes.

If you're paying attention to what you're sensing, you'll be able to make sense of it all. People who don't use the powerful senses that are built into all human beings—what you might call your *common* sense—may get all mixed up, and in frustration they may call what they are experiencing "nonsense."

That's a very clever play on words, but—

—it wasn't a "play" on words, it was the use of words quite accurately, to get across an important message: it may not serve humanity to dismiss what's being said here out of hand.

Okay. But how would we even know there are such Highly Evolved Beings helping us?

Don't worry, you'll know. You won't be able to miss it. You might call it something else, but you won't be able to miss it.

But if we call it something else, we won't know what it is.

It's not necessary to know what something is in order to benefit from it.

Have we already received such help? You've said we "won't be able to miss it." That puts it in the future tense. Are we just now starting to get this help?

You are just now becoming more aware of it.

But it's been there all along?

For what humans would call a very long time, yes.

So how helpful has it been, if it's gotten us to *this*?

Your species has actually come to *this* at exactly the perfect time and in the perfect way.

You've reached this Choice Point, and gained the ability to *see* it as exactly that, very quickly, in cosmic terms. And the conditions and circumstances that you abnegate are, in fact, *ideal*, in that they are now sufficiently startling to make your future options unmistakably clear.

So Highly Evolved Beings have worked very fast, actually, and very efficiently, measured by the clock of the universe.

8

Okay, this is getting *veeerrry* interesting. And I have to say, I totally "get" that Highly Evolved Beings could be watching over us. There have been enough UFO sightings over these past years to—

—these past years? You mean these past centuries—

—okay, these past centuries—to make it, one would think, incontrovertible that we're being observed. But helped? Stopped from hurting ourselves? How is *that* done? Planting ideas in our heads from afar? Okay, I can maybe even accept *that*, I can hold even that as a possibility . . . but actually visiting us?

We're getting into some pretty way out territory here.

Talk about a play on words.

And I didn't do that deliberately any more than you did. But I have to say, I never thought my conversation with God would carry me *here*. I never thought I'd get into *this*.

Remember when you said that we spent a significant portion of *Conversations with God, Book 3* talking about Highly Evolved Beings?

Yes, but not about them choosing to help us.

No, but about the fact that they exist, for sure.

Hypothetical existence and here-and-now assistance—including visiting us—are two different things. Two *dramatically* different things.

Agreed. Embracing this possibility is all part of the Third Invitation.

I thought the invitation was to awaken our species, not to be introduced to a *new* species. Are you now saying that to awaken the species I have to embrace a belief that other life forms . . .

. . . I guess most people would not call them HEBs, as we referred to Highly Evolved Beings in *Book 3*, but would just call them extraterrestrials . . .

. . . are you saying that I have to embrace a belief that extraterrestrials—

—let's just continue to call them Highly Evolved Beings, or HEBs for short—

—that an awakened species is choosing to help us, and is visiting us?

41

You don't *have to* embrace anything. You can move forward with your mission to awaken *your* species without adopting any belief that another species exists, much less the idea that there are Highly Evolved Beings choosing to help those on Earth.

But you just said that "embracing this is all part of the Third Invitation."

It's *part* of the invitation, it's not *required* to *accept* the invitation.

Would you unpack that for me?

Let's go back to the front door analogy.

If you knock on my door, and I open it and invite you in, and if I say, "How timely! I've just put out some hors d'oeuvres," that doesn't mean you may not accept the invitation unless you consume the specialty items on the tray.

Got it. I can come to the party without having to "swallow" what may not be my cup of tea—to mix metaphors.

You can, indeed.

I can accept the invitation to help awaken our species without having to believe that *other* species are choosing to help us, and are visiting us.

Yes. One decision does not hinge on the other.

That feels better. That feels like I've got a little more freedom here.

> Freedom is something you will *always* have. That's my promise to you. That is my eternal commitment.

I know, and I thank you. You've said that over and over, and I'm accepting that as your greatest gift to us.

So now let's say that I'm at least willing to explore these ideas that you've brought into our conversation. As a possibility. Let's say I'm willing to explore them as a possibility. What I really want to get to here is *how* I can help in awakening our species, and what an awakened humanity would look like—how it would create and experience life.

> I described that in detail—in great detail—in what you have called Book 3 of your conversation with me.

You did, and I'd love to have a look at that again. I've already forgotten most of what you said. It's amazing to me how we forget what would be really valuable for us to remember.

> Yes, that is part of the human experience, for sure. But repetition can help that. So we are going to summarize much of that again here—as well as repeating a few salient points from several of our other past conversations.

Okay by me. I can use the brush up, for sure. But right now I can't ignore the elephant in the room. I can't just pretend that you didn't say what you've just said right here.

You didn't just say that Highly Evolved Beings exist in the universe, you said that they are choosing to offer help to us directly—and that they are even visiting us.

As I observed earlier, those are two dramatically different pieces of information.

We can explore both. The second exploration will serve the first. It would be beneficial for many facets of life to be explored by you during this wonderful moment in the evolution of your species, with nothing assumed, and nothing eliminated from consideration.

Always keep your mind open. In all things, always keep your mind open. Everything is possible. Especially things you know nothing about. You wouldn't decide that something you know nothing about is impossible, would you?

Many humans manage to do that much of the time.

But you, and others like you, have been different. You've kept an open mind.

You're sitting here right now engaged in what others would call—what *many* others would call—an impossibility, a delusion, even a blasphemy. You're having a conversation with God. And you're thinking nothing of it.

Why should I? It was you who told me in prior conversations—speaking of our previous exchanges—to at least consider the *possibility* that there may be something I don't fully understand about Life and God, the understanding of which would change everything. So I've applied that to my experience.

I'm very clear now that all of us are totally capable of accessing the highest source of wisdom within us—which I call God—when we need or wish to.

We've all been doing it for years. Since we were born! Everybody is having a conversation with God all the time. Many just don't know it. Or they're calling it something else. That is, at least, *my* understanding, *my* observation, and *my* experience.

> So you can accept that *God* is communicating with you, but you're not so sure about Highly Evolved Beings helping you?

Good one. Good point. I guess the second idea seems a little more science-fiction-esque than the first, so it's one step removed from something I can easily and non-hesitatingly accept. I mean, even organized religion speaks of "revelations"—moments of wonderful clarity, insights presumably coming from God—but I don't hear much talk from pulpits about Highly Evolved Beings offering us guidance.

So it's a startling idea, and not one that's easy to step into without the slightest hesitation.

> Yet you'll find this as well in that part of our previous dialogue that you called Book 3.

Really? I've forgotten about that.

There I said: "When all in your race are led to mastery and achieve it, then your race as a whole (for your race *is* a whole) will move easily through time and space (you will have mastered the laws of physics as you understood them) and you will seek to assist those belonging to other races and other civilizations in coming to mastery as well."

And you replied: "Even as those of other races and other civilizations are doing so now, with us?"

To which I answered: "Exactly. Precisely."

So it shouldn't be a surprise to see this come up in our present exchange.

You know, I'd actually forgotten that you said that before.

My messages to you have been consistent through the years. What has not been consistent is your remembrance of them.

9

I'll be the first to acknowledge that remembering all that I know, and all the messages I have received from all the wonderful sources of wisdom in my life, has not been my high card; not my most highly developed attribute. It is with me as my father used to say: "So old so soon, so smart so late."

That said, I want to offer whatever energy I can to the global effort to awaken our species. So I'm so very happy to have been stimulated to enter into this present conversation.

But you know what? I like to think that I've added to that global effort already in my life. Many people have, just by the way they interact with others. So maybe I don't have to accept the Third Invitation. Maybe I already did so. Long ago.

Many of you have done, yes, some of the things that a person who has received and accepted and acted on this invitation might do, but most of you have not done so intentionally.

You've all done them graciously and generously and genuinely, but not with a specific intention behind them. And intention is everything. It sets the energetic signature for events that follow.

You can get in your car and drive down the road and be doing everything that a good driver would do, but if you haven't set your intention about where you're going, you'll find yourself getting nowhere.

I've had the experience.

But now, if you're saying that from this day forward your *intention* in everything you think, say, and do is to awaken your species—all as part of a self-expression that moves you forward on your own evolutionary journey—then you're going to see a different level of outcome.

This is what the Third Invitation is all about, and it is extended to everyone, not just to you. The conversation we are now having is for everyone who "accidentally" finds their way to it. You know who you are, because here you are.

The awakening of others will not happen by chance, or as a nice-but-not-specifically-focused-on result, but as an *intended effect* of the personal evolution of all those who self-select to accept the invitation that has been extended here.

A part of how you will all do this is by allowing your personal growth—and your struggles to achieve it—to be on display, to be modeled, publicly.

That's a big one. That's a huge thing to even contemplate.

Yet should you agree within to do it, you will have expanded the evolutionary impact of your day-to-day journey and moment-to-moment choices from Little You to Big You, from Local You to Universal You, from the Singular You to the Collective You.

By all of you allowing your personal evolutionary process to be observed by others, it can become a means by which the evolutionary process of all humanity is advanced.

And what a Perfect Time for Advancement this is.

But how could anyone even attempt to do this kind of thing without being tempted to feel *grandiose?* I wouldn't want to start deluding myself into thinking that I'm the hope of our species. And I wouldn't want to inadvertently take anyone else down that road either. Wouldn't I run the risk here of inadvertently placing myself into an artificially elevated mental state, where I could only be described as "manic," or even "deranged," thinking that I have this mission placed before me, and I am one of those who is going to carry it out?

Let's be clear. This is not about walking around declaring yourself to be the model of perfection and the example of evolutionary excellence. This is about simply not hiding your personal choices, but presenting yourself authentically to the world with regard to both your struggles and your progress as you seek to fully awaken.

If you really, genuinely, and humbly notice within that your personal, interior process is not focused on anyone else, and certainly not on "saving the world," but is only intended to move forward, as best you can, your own individual and personal evolution, and if you quietly share this with anyone who asks about your change of behavior—because others will notice it—you will not take yourself to the place you've described.

And if you really, genuinely, and humbly accept what you have called your own "so-called" imperfections (I see you as perfect just as you are, but we'll discuss that later), and you view yourself and declare yourself to be a person whose evolution is "in progress" and not anywhere near complete, you will also avoid the place you've described.

If you are clear that the purpose of your decision to accept the invitation to help awaken your species is not to set you up as some sort of leader, but to simply and humbly share that it is *you* who have been led, by a deep guidance from within, and now see that there is another way to be human—a way that humbly seeks to be more beneficial to yourself and others—you will never self-aggrandize.

Well, I certainly have enough imperfections to stop myself from imagining that I am some sort of spiritual "leader." Anyone who knows me will tell you that.

If you remain clear about that, you have nothing to worry about.

On the other hand, what I don't want to do, and what I don't want anyone else to do, is start to feel so bad about ourselves, *so* "imperfect" and *so* "unevolved," that we don't see ourselves as worthy of even trying to awaken (much less accept that we *are* awake)—to say nothing of helping to awaken others.

If you will allow yourself to see what you and others would call imperfections as part of what's perfect about all of you—and, by the way, see everyone else's "imperfections" in the same way—you will create a wonderful balance that will serve you and everyone else whose life you touch.

That balance will allow all of you who accept the Third Invitation to love yourselves just as you are, even as you humbly and genuinely seek to grow and further evolve every day. It will allow you also to give others permission to do the same.

You are a beautiful being, growing and evolving. As I have said many times before in our other conversations: If you saw you as God sees you, you would smile a lot.

I am so comforted every time I hear that. Thank you for saying it to me again.

You're welcome.

Now what I would really like to do is take that close-up glance at what living as an awakened species would look like—and how humans can create and experience life in a new way on Earth.

I want to go over again what you said in our previous conversations about how advanced beings from outer space live.

I will be happy to, but first you must understand that I am not talking about beings from "outer space" as you have defined it.

What do you mean "as I have defined it"? Outer space is *outer space.* It's the part of the cosmos that exists off this planet. It's the rest of the universe. That's how I define it. How do *you* define it?

Well, I'm going to quote your metaphysical master, William Shakespeare here:

"There are more things in Heaven and Earth, Horatio, than are dreamt of in your philosophy."

Which means?

Which means there are more things in what you call "outer space" than are dreamt of in your cosmology.

When you refer to "beings from outer space," you are referring to that part of the universe *of which you are aware.* Yet the universe is much larger and far more inter-dimensional than you may think.

Entities from the limited aspect of All That Exists that you call "outer space" are currently manifesting as physical entities, just as you are. And like humans, not all "beings from outer space" are peaceful, as I have already noted. Some are, and some are not.

Even those who *are* peaceful nevertheless occasionally behave violently, just as humans who see themselves as peaceful sometimes behave violently.

To put it mildly. Many humans kill other humans.

Exactly. So when I refer to beings who are choosing to help you, and when I describe the new way
humanity could choose to live based on how this
awakened species lives, I am referring to entities
who are not from the celestial realm in which beings
experience themselves as only or primarily physical.

You've got my attention.

I am referring to life forms existing in Another
Dimension.

A dimension where the entities are not physical?

A dimension where they *need* not be. A dimension where they can be, if they wish to be, if they
choose to "take on" what you would call a physical
form, but where doing so is not required for them to
have the experience for which all of life was created.

10

I'm intrigued by this, but I really want to have that review of what an awakened humanity could look like in terms of how it would create life on Earth, and we keep getting into these other areas . . .

I'm going to invite you to trust that it could be of benefit to explore these other areas first. It could be a means of helping you to understand where Highly Evolved Beings in the universe are "coming from" as they continue to create an experience that your species on Earth may choose to explore more deeply—and maybe even emulate.

Well, that places this diversion into a different context. Okay, fair enough. Then I'll ask: If the entities you refer to do not *need* to adopt a physical body, why would they ever bother doing it? God knows—you should excuse the expression, but God knows—I would never do it if I didn't have to.

Actually, you would, and have.

Do you think you are in physical form now because you *have* to be? Let me assure you that you are in physical form now because you *choose* to be.

This piece of information alone can change your whole way of being.

Why in the world would I choose *this?* If I could be free from all the unpleasant experiences of being in a body . . . why in the world would I choose not to do so?

You would choose not to do so if it served your purpose not to do so, and if you knew that you could be free from unpleasant experiences even while you are *in* a body.

I can?

Yes, and that's something that will become clear to you as this conversation continues. For right now, simply be aware that it is this which you do not know—which you do not remember—and that is why you cannot imagine choosing to be in a body if you do not have to be.

And you do *not* "have to be." You choose to be in physicality only when it serves your purpose. And right now it does, or you wouldn't be here. This is something that every Highly Evolved Being knows, and that you do not.

The problem is that you do not know what your purpose *is* (the vast majority of human beings do not remember), and so it *seems* to you as if you are in physical form against your will.

This affects your entire experience of being human. You think that you are not only in your body against your will, but that the things that you are observing and confronting while you are in your body are happening against your will. This has an enormous affect on the way you treat yourself and the way you effect others.

Helping human beings change the way they are with themselves and with each other—and thus change the future of life on Earth—is the reason all of you have been extended the Third Invitation.

When you have awakened yourself you will know, at last, what your purpose is—what your reason for being alive is, what the reason for all of *life* is. Then you can decide to express and experience that. And this will help and encourage others around you to work on themselves in the same way.

If you couldn't understand all of this, we wouldn't even be having this conversation. Nor would those who are following it right now be following it.

A point you made before.

A point I made before.

Those who have committed to their own full awakening, and to helping their dear fellow travelers on the planet do the same, have already self-identified.

They know, as you know and have said, that humanity is, in fact, One Decision Away from changing its future for the better forever, through the process of each person evolving to the next level, by embracing and demonstrating Who They Really Are.

And this is what Highly Evolved Beings are doing right now? In helping us to achieve that awakening, and by taking on a physical form in order to do it, they are expressing and experiencing Who They Really Are? Is that what I am to get from all this?

> Yes. That is precisely the reason that the beings I am referring to would choose to take on a physical form.
>
> A difference between your species and theirs is that they are moving back and forth between physical and metaphysical states at will, whereas most of you imagine that you are doing so in a way that has nothing to do with your will.
>
> That's why I've allowed you to get into all of this here. Changing this thought that you are moving between the physical and the metaphysical against your will is going to be a big part of your personal transformation.
>
> You now describe your movement from the physical to the metaphysical with the term "death," and you have it in your mind that this is the worst thing that could ever happen to you. Yet this event is merely one step in your ongoing evolutionary process.

We actually *fear* the process by which we continue to evolve. We profoundly fear disembodiment—what we call "death"—and thus seek to avoid it at all cost.

> Literally, *at all cost*—including the abandoning of your consciousness, of what you "know to be so," and of your deepest inner awareness.

In this you fail to recognize that you are already awake. You abandon your Self in order to "save" yourself.

This is the irony of the behavior of every very young sentient species. It is the supreme irony of your present human experience.

Yet you are starting to understand now. You are beginning to awaken, and you are ready to accept the invitation to awaken others. But you cannot awaken others unless you know what you are awakening *to*.

That is the purpose of this diversion. It is to let you know that you are awakening to the awareness that you are in your present body deliberately, not as a trial and a tribulation, not as something from which you can't wait to escape, but as a way to experience and demonstrate what only physical life on Earth can offer you the greatest opportunity to express.

Well, let me explain why this whole experience here very often *does* seem like a trial and a tribulation.

If I am understanding all of this correctly, these HEBs you are talking about are moving between the physical and metaphysical states instantly. They embody and dis-embody on the spot, when and as they wish. We humans, on the other hand, seem to be required to go through a period of time in the physical—for some it may be very short, maybe even just a moment, while for others it may be many years—but time passes.

What's more, on every occasion when humans move from the metaphysical back into the physical, they have to "start life over." We have to embody as babies, and learn the basics of being in a body all over again.

I don't hear you saying that this is required of Highly Evolved Beings from Another Dimension. You're saying they can change from one form of expression to another spontaneously, and move from the "nonphysical" to the "physical" as fully developed beings, not as beings at the beginning of a physical life cycle.

Do I have all of this right? If so, that would be a major plus, for sure. We're at a huge disadvantage here, having to "start over" every time we want to "physicalize," and having to confront all of the difficulties and overcome all of the challenges of years of day-to-day life.

Actually, you're under no disadvantage at all. You're doing exactly what you want to do.

If would be beneficial for you to understand that you are physicalizing for a different reason than HEBs. You are physicalizing because you *want* the experience of growing from embryo to infancy to childhood to adolescence to adulthood to old age. And you want it more than once.

You've come back into the Realm of the Physical over and over again in order to embrace the fullness of this experience, because you seek to understand *all of it,* thoroughly and completely, thus to both create and experience who you are from every angle, through every lens, in every circumstance and situation.

As you move through this process of self-creation, you have been all of it in your lifetimes. The victim and the villain, the strong and the weak, the oppressed and the oppressor, the so-called "right" and the so-called "wrong," the so-called "good" one and the so-called "evil" one.

I thought there was no such thing as "right" and "wrong." I thought that none of us were "good" or "bad" in God's eyes.

Your thought is accurate. These are labels that *you* have given to certain behaviors, not that God has applied. God loves you and adores you and embraces you through all your processes of "becoming," of "growing," of self-realization.

I desire for *you* to decide who you choose to be and how you wish to experience that—so that you might know Who You Really Are not through having been told or assigned or ordered, but rather, through having *created* your Self in that way, given all the options, offered all the choices, presented with every possibility.

Now you have known the power and the glory of being Divine—through the *freedom* and the *will* to be Divine.

This is Divinity *expressed*, not simply *bestowed*. This is Godliness *experienced*—and that has been my purpose in creating life Itself.

And so, you have been the here and the there of it, the up and the down of it, the left and the right of it, the big and the small of it, the fast and the slow of it, the shallow and the deep of it, the light and the dark of it, and yes, the young and the old of it.

You're using physicality to know and experience all of it—every conceivable expression—by producing a Contextual Field within which you may choose who and how you wish to be.

This Contextual Field is the greatest blessing of your life in this dimension, because in the absence of That Which You Are Not, that which You Are is not.

That is, it is not experienceable.

In the absence of dark, light is not. In the absence of small, big is not. In the absence of fast, slow is not. And in the absence of what you have called "bad," what you have called "good" is not.

Therefore, judge not and neither condemn, but be a light *unto* the darkness, that you might announce and declare, express and fulfill, know and experience Who You Really Are—and that all others whose lives you touch might know who *they* really are as well, by the power of your example.

Is this not what all masters have done?

You have said these words to me many times before. Still, within this present context, they make even more sense to me, ring even more true. But why wouldn't this be true also for Highly Evolved Beings?

As just noted, HEBs do not embody for this reason. They have already experienced physicality fully. They have done so to completion. So they do not "start over" in each embodiment, unless it serves them to do so in a particular physicalization.

What does that mean?

If a Highly Evolved Being enters into physical form in its dimension, it is because that HEB wishes to recreate and re-experience something that cannot be created or experienced in the metaphysical state. "Starting over" from an initial embodiment state is rarely required in order to do this.

If a Highly Evolved Being enters into physical form *not* in its dimension, it is because that HEB wishes to offer assistance to sentient beings in the Realm of the Physical in the understanding, expressing, and full experiencing of themselves as who they really are. HEBs may then choose to "start over" in a life cycle as they physicalize.

But why would HEBs even choose to offer assistance to sentient beings in a dimension other than their own?

So they may continue to express and fulfill, know and experience who *they* really are, at the next level—and the next, and the next, and the next. HEBs are choosing to experience and express themselves not as The Seeker, but as The Answer.

The whole universe, the entire cosmos in each of its dimensions, is filled with sentient beings, each imbued with the exact same desire—the desire to express and experience their True Nature and their True Identity.

This involves a process of, first, moving through and knowing every aspect of being physical. Then moving through and knowing every aspect of being metaphysical. Then, integrating both.

And here is the great secret that Highly Evolved Beings are focusing their energies on sharing: Full integration can occur at any moment. The process can be condensed. An entire civilization can begin living as an awakened species whenever it wishes.

11

Okay! It's time to know how to do that!

I'm grateful for having been given the opportunity to get to a place where my mind can at least feel more clear about how all this could have happened, but I am ready to move forward now.

If we are being invited to awaken the species, I wish to know *to what*. What is the Way of Being to which we might invite everyone to awaken?

Are we supposed to simply embrace and adopt the principles and practices, understandings and behaviors of a totally different civilization living in a different dimension? Can't we achieve a better life as individuals, and a better tomorrow as a global collective, using the highest values of humanity?

> You certainly can. But it may be helpful and beneficial to you to think in terms of different energies, not different civilizations. This whole question of what makes life work wonderfully, joyously and masterfully is not a matter of "local customs," it is a matter of universal truth regarding life's fundamental energy.

There is only one energy or essence in the cosmos, and that is what you have called, in human language, Love.

The ideas that Highly Evolved Beings have sought to place before humanity are simply thoughts about how to live and love in a way that is more beneficial to your species, and will give each individual a chance to advance in their personal evolution more quickly.

HEBs don't assert that their way of living is "right" for humans. They simply offer you the opportunity to decide for yourself. This is their way of helping you, even as you may seek to help others to awaken.

So it may be of benefit to take a look at these ideas, see if or where you may find a contrast with human behaviors, and decide if you choose to try some new ways of being human.

I agree. And I already know there will be contrasts . . . so tell me what the biggest difference is. I mean, let's cut to the chase here.

The most striking and significant difference is that Highly Evolved Beings are utterly and completely, absolutely and entirely without violence of any kind.

They do not engage in physical violence, they do not project verbal violence, they do not even momentarily entertain violence in their thoughts.

They do not call violence "self-defense," they do not call it "entertainment," and they certainly do not call it "sport."

They simply cannot justify or support the inflicting of physical or emotional pain—not even the slightest discomfort—on any other entity.

Is there a formula by which they have been able to achieve this? What do they know that we don't know that opens the way for them to be like that?

All violence has disappeared from their culture because all anger has disappeared from their reality.

And that is because . . . ?

It is because they live in the knowing that they have *nothing to lose* by being good and kind and caring and compassionate and unselfish and giving and accepting and unconditionally loving in every instant of every moment of every circumstance or situation.

They know that they cannot lose their life for any reason or in any way, nor can they lose anything else of value to them, because nothing else *is* of value to them other than life itself, their very existence—which they understand is what provides them with the opportunity for the only experience they desire.

Which is?

The experience of their Divinity.

So these beings cannot be killed? Not even by an outward circumstance having nothing to do with being violent with each other? Like a Black Hole (just to make something up here) swallowing their civilization's home?

> There is no outward circumstance within the physical universe that could cause them to equate the changing of their manifested form to losing their life or ending their existence.

So moving from the physical into the non-physical isn't seen by them as the end of anything.

> That's exactly right. They know that they will always exist and never cease to be, no matter what happens to their physically manifested forms.
>
> That includes a "black hole" swallowing any planet on which they may happen to be embodying.

When you do not fear losing your life, ever, you have no reason to ever become violent? What about losing something, or not being able to get something, you desire?

> You have already been told, by masters on your planet, that desire that you feel must be satiated is the cause of all suffering. And suffering is the cause of all violence. Eliminate suffering and violence goes away, evaporates, dissolves, disappears.

If you're fully awakened, if you're a Highly Evolved Being, you escape all desires?

> You escape the incapacitation of desires. You escape the ruination of being ruled by your desires.

When you know that your life will never end, you know that anything you wish to experience you have an eternity to create—or to recreate if you've had it once and wish to experience it again.

There's a saying in the cosmos: Eternal Life brings Eternal Peace.

If, on the other hand, you imagine that you have a *limited* time in which to experience what you desire to experience, you will give up your peace to acquire it, or to hold onto it if and when you do acquire it.

That's the story of humanity in fifty words or less, for sure. So life for HEBs from Another Dimension is felt as an eternal reality.

It *is* an eternal reality. Life is an eternal experience for *all* sentient beings, but few sentient beings who think of themselves and express themselves primarily as a physical body experience their eternality as a felt reality. They experience their *physicality* as their felt reality, and they imagine that when their physicality is over, their existence has come to an end.

At best, they hold the idea of eternal life as a concept, a theory, a doctrine or belief; as something that "might be," but about which they are not sure.

Because the fully awakened entities I have been talking about exist and have their being in Another Dimension, they are *certain* that life is eternal.

Sure they are, because it's easy for them! They are *experiencing* it, not just thinking about it or praying about it or hoping about it. And they *have* been experiencing it since . . . well, since *forever*.

> So have you. The difference is, they know it and you don't. They remember it.

Can we remember it? How can all of *us* remember it?

> What do you think you are doing here?

12

Nonviolence is a striking contrast between Highly Evolved Beings and humans, and I understand that their awareness of life as an eternal experience can certainly create a context within which violence would be seen as unnecessary. Might there, however, be a more "practical" means of reducing or even eliminating violence from the human experience?

We've tried for several millennia to convince member of our species that their life is eternal. Even with this idea having been accepted by many, it doesn't seem to have reduced violence in any significant way.

> There *is* a practical way to eliminate violence. Simply move away from humanity's present deep belief in Separation.

Ah, yes, this I "get" immediately. And I don't have to be helped by Highly Evolved Beings from another realm to do so. All I have to do is look around me.

I observe that right now most people who believe in God—and that is by far the largest number of people on our planet—still embrace a Separation Theology. Their way of looking at God is that humans are "over here" and God is "over there."

This would not matter if it began and ended there, but the problem with a Separation Theology is that it produces a Separation Cosmology—that is, a way of looking at all of Life which says that everything is separate from everything else.

This wouldn't be so bad if it was just a point of view, but the problem is that a Separation Cosmology produces a Separation Psychology—that is, a psychological viewpoint which says that I am "over here" and everyone else is "over there."

This would also be something we could live with if that was all there was to it, but the problem is that a Separation Psychology produces a Separation Sociology—that is, a way of socializing with each other which encourages everyone within human society to act as separate entities serving their own separate interests.

Now we've entered into truly dangerous territory, because a Separation Sociology inevitably produces a Separation Pathology—pathological behaviors of self-destruction, engaged in individually and collectively, and producing suffering, conflict, violence, and death by our own hands—evidenced everywhere on our planet throughout human history.

To me it seems that only when our Separation Theology is replaced by a Oneness Theology will our pathology be healed. A Oneness Theology would recognize that we have been *differentiated* from God, but not *separated* from God, even as the fingers on our hand are differentiated but not separated from each other, but connected by the hand itself, and by the hand to the entire body—even as we are differentiated but not separated, connected by being parts of the body of God.

> You have put this all perfectly. This is shared with great clarity.

Well, it all came from you, of course. And now, we are being encouraged once again—as we have been in every one of the prior *Conversations with God* exchanges with you—to understand that all of Life is One Thing.

> Yes. This is what Highly Evolved Beings from the Other Dimension not only understand, but experience.
> They not only know that life is eternal, they know that there is no separation in the universe— of *anything* from *anything*. This awareness is a pillar of their way of life; it is the foundation of their civilization.

For us, then, this is the first step that will be taken when we become an awakened species. And we haven't even taken that first step, after all these years—all these *millennia*—on our planet.

> It is the most important step you could take right now. Do not discourage yourself with what you haven't done, encourage yourself with what you will do.

I sure hope that we do, because I can see that embracing this idea as a functional reality would be the beginning of the end of how things are on our planet right now. It would be the start of a new creation, of a new tomorrow. It would become the New Cultural Story of Humanity.

I want to run out and tell everybody: *Oneness is not a characteristic of life. Life is a characteristic of oneness.*

> That would be a very powerful message to share.
> And powerfully put.

Yes. This is what we have not understood about our existence on Earth, the understanding of which would change everything.

Life is the expression of oneness itself. God is the expression of Life Itself. God and Life are one. We are a part of Life. We do not and cannot stand outside of it. Therefore we are a part of God. It is a circle. It cannot be broken.

> Your understanding of this is identical to that of Highly Evolved Beings from Another Dimension. And you are not the only one on Earth who is clear about this.
>
> All it takes now is for all of those who are equally clear to self-identify, then to commit to joining in a global undertaking to awaken the species.

But not to do so in such a grandiose way that it defeats their purpose, as no one will listen to them.

> It is good that you keep returning to this. It would indeed defeat your purpose if you set yourself apart as "Those Who Know," and decide that it is your job to tell others what they don't know.

Your mission would be to tell others that they *do* know—and they simply may not *know* that they know.

This is a gentle sharing, a gentle awakening, not such a startling jolt that all anyone wants to do is go back to sleep.

Okay, so I see that this single change is but another articulation of the One Decision I spoke of earlier. It could quickly bring about a new way of living on Earth. That excites me. The possibilities that arise from this excite me.

I'm still trying, though, to get sense of more than just one or two ways that our daily experience here would change, as a practical matter, if we moved through every-day life in the way that these Highly Evolved Beings have been encouraging us to do.

I can give you a list of them.

Please do.

13

You may want to memorize this. Or at least put it in a place where you will see it often.

1. An awakened species sees the Unity of All Life and lives into it. Humans in an unawakened state often deny it or ignore it.

2. An awakened species tells the truth, always. Humans in an unawakened state too often lie, to themselves as well as others.

3. An awakened species says one thing and will do what they say. Humans in an unawakened state often say one thing and do another.

4. An awakened species, having seen and acknowledged what is so, will always do what works. Humans in an unawakened state often do the opposite.

5. An awakened species does not embrace a principle in its civilization that correlates with the concepts that humans refer to as "justice" and "punishment."

6. An awakened species does not embrace a principle in its civilization that correlates with the concept that humans refer to as "insufficiency."

7. An awakened species does not embrace a principle in its civilization that correlates with the concept that humans refer to as "ownership."

8. An awakened species shares everything with everyone all the time. Humans in an unawakened state often do not, only sharing with others in limited circumstances.

9. An awakened species creates a balance between technology and cosmology; between machines and nature. Humans in an unawakened state often do not.

10. An awakened species would never under any circumstances terminate the current physical expression of another sentient being unless asked directly by that other being to do so. Humans in an unawakened state often kill other humans without that other human requesting them to.

11. An awakened species would never do anything that could potentially damage or harm the physical environment that supports the members of the species when they are physicalized. Humans in an unawakened state often do so.

12. An awakened species never poisons itself. Humans in an unawakened state often do so.

13. An awakened species never competes. Humans in an unawakened state are often in competition with each other.

14. An awakened species is clear that it needs nothing. Humans in an unawakened state often create a need-based experience.

15. An awakened species experiences and expresses unconditional love for everyone. Humans in an unawakened state often cannot imagine even a Deity who does this, much less do they do it themselves.

16. An awakened species has harnessed the power of metaphysics. Humans in an unawakened state often largely ignore it.

There are more differences, of course, but those are some of the chief characteristics of an awakened species, and the major differences between such a species and humanity in its present unawakened state.

Gosh, part of me feels that this list is an indictment of our whole species, our whole away of life.

Is it an "indictment" of a three-year-old to observe that adults understand things she does not?

Celebrate that you know what you know! Celebrate that you clearly see the difference between your behaviors and behaviors that you may decide are more beneficial.

Celebrate the growth of knowing this, even as
you celebrate the early steps of every child.

Thanks for reminding me. You keep making this point. We really are a very young species. Perhaps we should drive that point home in specific terms, so it can become real in people's minds.

A lot of folks like to think of humans as highly evolved. In fact, humanity has just emerged from its *infancy* on this planet. In their book, *New World New Mind,* Robert Ornstein and Paul Ehrlich placed this in perspective in one mind-boggling paragraph:

"Suppose Earth's history were charted on a single year's calendar, with midnight January 1 representing the origin of the Earth and midnight December 31 the present. Then each day of Earth's 'year' would represent 12 million years of actual history. On that scale, the first form of life, a simple bacterium, would arise sometime in February. More complex life-forms, however, come much later; the first fishes appear around November 20. The dinosaurs arrive around December 10 and disappear on Christmas Day. The first of our ancestors recognizable as human would not show up until the *afternoon of December 31.* Homo sapiens—our species—would emerge at around 11:45 p.m. . . . and all that has happened in recorded history would occur in the final minute of the year."

That puts things into perspective beautifully.
And it creates a context within which it can now be
understood why, in human societies, most people
deny much of what they see. They even deny their
personal feelings, and, eventually, their own truth.

But what's been said here now, repeatedly, about how early in our development we are as a species gives me great hope, as I said once before. I'm seeing wonderful, wonderful days ahead—both for us individually and for humanity collectively—as we mature and grow into our potential.

> That is the great opportunity that awaits you. It is just over the horizon.

Yes, this *is* the Perfect Time for Advancement! But do we have to wait—I think I already know the answer to this, but I'm going to ask anyway—do we have to wait until the whole human race, or the majority of our species, awakens before any of us can experience living as a Highly Evolved Being? Because it could be a long, long wait until most humans get to that place.

> You're right, you do already know the answer to this. Not only do you not have to wait—you are not *supposed* to wait.
>
> History is now watching to see who on Earth will choose to self-select as being committed to modeling these behaviors and, by their words and actions, join in a global movement to awaken their species.
>
> Who on Earth will celebrate fully their True Nature, and who will joyously co-create the wonderful days that lie ahead when they do so?

14

I'm won over. I see now how much of this information about Highly Evolved Beings can be useful and can help us as we work to awaken ourselves—or as you put it, to allow ourselves to know that we already are awake—and to help awaken the species.

I feel I want to go out now and share many of these principles—which, as you've pointed out, are not "other worldly," but simply grander notions of how to love. First, I want to practice living them, then I want to share them with others.

And I would love it if you would first offer a short commentary exploring some of the points on that list, so that I can know what this all can "look like" in real terms as I seek to live them and share them in real life.

I will be happy to. Let's start at the top of the list.

#1. An awakened species sees the Unity of All Life and lives into it. Humans in an unawakened state often deny it or ignore it.

Highly Evolved Beings never question that all things are One Thing; they know experientially that there is only One Thing, and all things are part of the One Thing there is.

Because they exist in another dimension, they can actually see this visually, not just conceptually. They are able to view the sub-molecular structure of all things.

They observe that there is only one energy in the universe—one Source or Force—and that this Source or Force simply mixes up the foundational elements of which It is comprised, adding some and subtracting others, then alters the vibrational frequency of those variously combined elements, to generate differing expressions of the Essential Essence.

I have called these differing expressions Singularizations of The Singularity.

Which is a great name for them, because that is exactly what they are. All things in existence are created through this alchemy, which produces the "recipe" for the universal soup.

The elements are attracted to each other through the conscious choice-making of each element, impacted as they are by the combined energy of the Essential Essence comprising what we will call your soul.

Wait a minute. "Consciousness" exists at the elemental level???

Of course. What you call the elemental level *is* consciousness. It is Consciousness in Action.

Every cell of your body acts with intelligence. You can't so much as cut your little finger without creating a cellular rush to the site of the injury to repair the damage. *You think the cells of your body don't know what they are doing—and why?*

And I tell you, every element of the universe is imbued with this foundational intelligence.

Oh, my God.

Precisely.

Can they talk to each other? Okay, "talk" is a funny word to use here. I am actually asking, can the cells of the body communicate element-to-element?

Of course they can. What do you think "thought" is?

"Thoughts" are cells communicating with one another?

That is exactly what they are. Do you know how brain cells work?

Yes, but when you talk about the brain you're talking about neurons and peptides and somas and dendrites and all that stuff. The cells throughout our body are not like the cells of the brain.

They aren't? Who told you that?

Let me repeat: every ounce of life is imbued with foundational intelligence. Read that: *every cell, every particle, every sub-molecular element, in the universe.*

Then there must be a way that I can get the cells of my body to do whatever I communicate that I want them to do! Like heal me from an illness, for instance.

> You are right if you are suggesting that the energy of your thoughts has an influence over the cells of your body.

I remember learning of Émile Coué, a French psychologist and pharmacist who introduced in the early part of the 20th century a process of psychotherapy with a foundation in optimistic and conscious autosuggestion. As an experiment he invited people who were ill to repeat at least twenty times a day—and especially in the morning and before retiring—a simple mantra: *Tous les jours à tous points de vue je vais de mieux en mieux.* In English: *Every day, in every way, I am getting better and better.*

> And his results?

A remarkable percentage of his patients got better!

> Of course.

My heavens, can it then be possible to get most of the cells of the body to choose the same thing most of the time?

> Ah! This is the same question you are asking yourselves right now regarding the rest of the people on the planet.

It is! It is this same question *exactly.*

And the answer is, it is possible, through *alignment*.

The choice to act co-jointly, in unison and in harmony with each other, is made by elements of life when there is alignment on purpose within the sector or area where those elements exist.

The cells of your body will act in unison and in harmony with each other when there is alignment with the soul on the direction each moment in your life will take, from a cellular level, based on the soul's agenda in that femtosecond.

Okay, I had to look that one up. A "femtosecond" is one quadrillionth, or one millionth of one billionth, of a second.

Exactly. And your soul is The Source of the energy of the Essential Essence that resides with you.

The soul is "God in us."

It is indeed. Not just in thought, not just in word, but in deed. The soul is the expression, now individualized, of the "being" that is God. It is God "being" manifested.

In our case on Earth, the soul is God being a human, and a human is a soul being God!

Exactly! Precisely! Absolutely! Positively! Manifestly! You have said it perfectly.

Wow, this is really getting us more deeply into metaphysics than I ever thought I'd go, but I've got to ask: Are you telling me that every sub-molecular particle of every expression of life in the universe has to be *talked into something* in order to do it? Are you saying that the tiniest particle of energy has the consciousness to make *decisions* by evaluating *choices* arising out of *alternatives* placed before it?

Man, this is too much. Forget about the rest of the people on the planet, how do I even get all the parts of *me* to agree on doing the same thing!?

> That's the question, isn't it . . .
> That's the biggest question of all time.
> But it's actually easier than you think.

Monsieur Coué says it's actually as easy *as* I think!

> And that is the biggest secret of life. When you understand this, you've moved to a place of mastery.

Okay, so tell me how this works, metaphysically. I've been told a thousand times about the power of our thoughts, but how does this work, what makes this work, metaphysically?

> You told me, and I know, that you have an insatiable mind, but do you really want to get into the alchemy of the universe?

15

I really haven't *planned* this conversation; I'm just noticing that it's going where it's going. I don't want to put off for too long the rest of our deeper exploration of that list you gave us, but this is too fascinating for me to pass up. Can we just look at this briefly?

Okay, then. Obviously, this could fill an entire book, but here is Metaphysics 101: A Short Course in Ultimate Reality.

As we've noted a while back in this conversation, all elements of life are imbued with what you would call, in your language, "intelligence"—or Awareness of Its Inherent Function.

This Awareness fills each element to its maximum capacity. That is, every element is imbued with Divine Intelligence utterly, full out, from border to border. Indeed, it would not be incorrect to say that the element itself IS this intelligence, in particle form.

So each element of life, down to the tiniest submolecular particle, is a part of the Mind of God.

With your sense of poetry, that would be how you would put it . . . and I have no reason to argue with you.

Now the Elements of the Essential Essence are attracted to each other by an aspect or characteristic that you would call, in human terms, "common function."

That is, they are *all trying to do something*. And it is *the same thing*. They are all in action, forever moving, continuously vibrating—but not without purpose.

Their purpose is simply to BE. They realize that life is movement. If movement ever stops, that which you call life would not exist.

Life = Motion = Life.

Yes.

Now, as to what each *element* wants to be, *that doesn't matter*. The individual element does not have a preference in the matter. It simply wants to exist. Its desire is to "be."

What is called "alignment," then—and the subsequent joint or unified action to which you refer— is created by the vibrational influence of any force larger than an individual element.

It is this way throughout all of nature. The larger the force, the more "pull" it has on every smaller element within its Impact Area. So every element within any Impact Area will fall into alignment with the larger force that is pulling on it.

No one has ever said this to me in this way. Why can't this be explained in this simple way to every child?

It can. And in the civilizations of Highly Evolved Beings it is. This awareness is shared with every emerging entity, each of whom is told about the Oneness of Life and the Circle of Life.

So if you as creative beings wish all the elements of life, down into the tiniest particle, to move in a particular direction, you must create alignment using the force of combined energy focused in a particular way.

And *thought* is that force.

Then what creates that focus? How do we cause energy—that is, *thought*—to be focused in a particular way?

Desire.

Desire exists in the soul. It is the soul, defined in one word. The soul is the local expression of God's desire—which is to experience Itself.

Desire is the creator of intention. Intention is the creator of thought. Thought is the creator of action. Action is the creator of outcome.

Not all thought, however, is created by the intention arising out of the soul's desire. Thought can also, in a sense, have a "mind of its own." That is, the energy impulse that produces a thought can arise out of the body's desires.

This produces a different kind of action, which can generate a totally different outcome than the soul had in mind. The soul *put* its intended outcome in your mind, but your body made you go *out of your mind* for a moment.

This is what happens when you think you are a body, as opposed to knowing that you are a soul.

Most of us only hope that we *have* a soul, or *believe* that we have a soul, but do not know for sure. But we *are* sure that we have a body—so this is what most of us think of ourselves as.

Once again, you're pulling this all together beautifully. That's the way to put the puzzle pieces into place.

Now every element of the Essential Essence—from the individual soul to every individual energy unit in the body (and in the universe)—is imbued with Desire, which is a particular form or expression of energy, in direct proportion of its size.

The smallest elements have the smallest Desire. Larger elements, which are created by the smallest elements being drawn to them, coalescing and thus producing them, have greater Desire.

The amount of Desire existing within any given element of life will be found to exist in direct proportion to that element's size. Think of Desire as the spark plug in the engine of Life.

So if what we call "God" is everything that *is*, that would make God's Desire the biggest Desire of all.

Correct. Again, very insightful. And God's Desire is that every sentient being—that is, every element of life large enough and sophisticated or complex enough to reflect self-awareness—has the ability to create its own reality, using Free Will and Conscious Choice.

This is an alchemic way of saying that the Foundational Elements of Life—the tiny individual particles of the Essential Essence—have no preference in the matter of how the *combination* of elements align.

Your soul, which is a collection of such particles, does have an intention. Your soul is the local presence of the Divine Intention, which is to express Divinity in every moment *as each sentient being defines it.*

This being has the freedom to create whatever it chooses, which is Godliness in its grandest demonstration. Or to put this all still another way: You all have Free Will.

You will note that I have been saying to you from the very first conversation we ever had that with regard to how your life is lived, God has no preference in the matter. My only Desire is that *your* preference be empowered.

Therefore that which "matters"—that is, that which you cause to turn from pure energy into solid matter—is up to you, individually and collectively. In making this choice, you can either listen to your body, to your mind, or to your soul.

And that is Metaphysics 101: A Short Course in Ultimate Reality.

16

Golly, there are so many implications to all this, and I could talk with you about it forever, but I do want to look at some of the other items on that list, so that we can know what we're talking about as we seek to rouse ourselves from our long sleep—

—and from your more recent experience of being awake but not knowing it, or not acting like it—

—yes, and as we then humbly hope to awaken others. Let's move now to Item #2, may we?

Yes. #2 says: An awakened species tells the truth, always. Humans in an unawakened state too often lie, to themselves as well as others.

For instance, you would have a hard time convincing a Highly Evolved Being that the constant stream of sounds and images you place before your offspring in their youngest years has absolutely no effect on their ideas about life, and therefore nothing to do with how your next generation creates its daily experience.

You, on the other hand, *can't* admit that the increasing violence in your society arises, at least in part, from the continual onslaught of such images, because if you did, you would have to do something about it. And you think there is nothing you *can* do about it, so it is better to ignore it.

Yes, we've talked several times now about television programs and movies and video games and Internet sites, and even children's *toys* that depict—and even encourage our offspring to use as forms of "play"—enactments of violence, violence, *violence* at every turn.

And yet you imagine yourselves to be—or, worse yet, allow yourselves to be—powerless to do anything about any of this.

Some of us do the same thing with tobacco. Or a constant diet of unhealthy food. Or a lack of exercise. Or the societal values that drive our human experience toward constant conflict.

This business of looking straight at self-damaging behaviors and doing nothing about them is the mark of sentient beings who do not care enough about themselves, or do not understand enough about themselves, to *do* enough *for* themselves to stop the harm they are doing *to* themselves.

You might expect a four-year-old child to act like this, but not his forty-year-old parents. So we have to grow up at least a little and see the truth, then *speak* the truth about what we see.

That would be a good start, yes.

And Highly Evolved Beings never hide from, always see, and unfailingly tell, the truth.

Yes. An awakened species is incapable of lying, given its combined intention. Its members have learned that self-deceit and deceit of others is utterly non-productive, moving them away from, rather than toward, their jointly held desires and intentions.

It would be virtually impossible for a Highly Evolved Being to communicate an untruth in any event, because its individual vibration would alter in such a way as to make it apparent that what the entity was communicating was not in sync with what it knows and understands.

Like when we blush—some of us, anyway—if we try to lie.

Very *much* like that, yes, only at a higher level. The whole entity itself would shake and vibrate at such a variant speed that the truth would literally be shaken out of it. So there would be no point in trying to lie to begin with.

Notice that when humans do hold jointly held desires and intentions, they do not lie to each other. Lying is an announcement that you want something other than the person you are lying to. This may seem obvious to you, but what may not be so obvious is how to eliminate this.

The end of deceit will come with the end of separation. When your culture and your civilization decides that there really is only one of you, in a multiplicity of forms, and therefore only one desire, there will thereafter be only one intention.

And that desire will be?

To reach completion in the expression in every moment of what every living entity desires.

Which is?

Once again, as mentioned before: The experience of itself as the only thing it really is. Divinity. Or, to use the word in your language that was mentioned before: Love. The energy that you call "love."

The unity of the universe is God's expression of Divine Love for all of life in all of its forms.

17

I'd love to hear your commentary on Item #3.

#3: An awakened species says one thing and will do what they say. Humans in an unawakened state often say one thing and do another.

Human beings also do not always say what they think. For Highly Evolved Beings not to communicate what they're holding in thought—which is different, by the way, than outright lying—would be seen as a behavior without benefit.

What good is holding a thought if it is not expressed? And for Highly Evolved Beings not to follow through on what they say to each other or to themselves that they will do, would be viewed as equally without benefit.

What if the thought I'm holding is not very nice?

Why would you hold a thought that's not very nice? Stop that. Sometimes you'll have a thought that runs through your mind, but you don't have to hold it there.

What if I can't help it?

I beg your pardon? You imagine that you *can't help what you're holding onto?* No wonder your species is in such trouble!

Yes, I know. And I *have* changed a *lot* of the way I think. But still, not every thought that runs through my head is worth sharing with another.

Then don't. Only share the thoughts that you hold onto.

By the way, you do know, don't you, that every thought you hold onto is a prayer?

No pressure.

Actually, there *is* none for Highly Evolved Beings. All they do is immediately change their mind if they experience a thought moving through their mind that they don't wish to manifest.

If they have any fleeting negative idea at all, they *don't give it a second thought.*

After a while of doing this, they've trained their mind never to consider for more than a nanosecond any thoughts that they do not wish to see begin to take shape in their reality. They just don't hold onto them. They let them go immediately, and move to a new and more positive thought.

You might call this a New Thought Movement, and you could join in groups that choose to engage in this very practice.

Yes, you've said that to me before.

And I'll do so again, no doubt, if it serves the moment at hand.

So keep new thoughts moving through your mind if a passing thought is anything but positive. Then, when the thought you are holding is positive, yes, of course feel free to share it with anyone who it might concern, or who might have a reason to be interested.

As for saying one thing and doing what you say, let your word be your bond. And if you don't think you'll be likely, or able, to do what you're now thinking of saying . . . *don't say it.*

If on the other hand you meant it when you said what you would do, but find later that you really can't because something has happened that has intervened, then go to anyone and everyone to whom you said this thing, and clear it up with them. Tell them the truth. Humbly and gently explain why you won't be able to do what you said.

Tell the truth to everyone about everything. That's how Highly Evolved Beings live.

I'm seeing that these first few items are related at some level. For instance, Item #4 ties right into this.

Yes. Item #4 says: An awakened species, having seen and acknowledged what is so, will always do what works. Humans in an unawakened state often do the opposite.

This feels a lot like Items #1, #2, and #3, only from a different angle.

Can you give me examples of how Item #4 relates to everyday life on Earth, so that I can get closer to the impact of this on us?

> Certainly. And because these first few items are related, you have already made note of some of this, but let's bring it all together here.
>
> If your objective is to live a life of peace, joy, and love, *violence does not work*. This has *already been demonstrated*.
>
> If your objective is to live a life of good health and great longevity, consuming dead flesh daily, smoking known carcinogens continuously, and drinking gallons of nerve-deadening, brain-frying liquids like alcohol regularly *does not work*. This has *already been demonstrated*.
>
> If your objective is to raise offspring free of violence and rage, placing them directly in front of vivid depictions of violence and rage during their most impressionable years *does not work*. This has *already been demonstrated*.
>
> If your objective is to care for Earth and wisely husband her resources, acting as if those resources are limitless *does not work*. This has *already been demonstrated*.
>
> If your objective is to discover and cultivate a relationship with a loving Deity so that religion can make a difference in the affairs of humans, then teaching of a god of righteousness, punishment,

and terrible retribution *does not work*. This has *already been demonstrated.*

Do you need any more examples?

No, I get the picture.

I like the way all of these tie together. I mean, one thing just naturally leads to another. It would be a lot easier for humans to stop saying one thing and doing another if they fixed the first tendencies. Namely, their tendency to see everything and everyone as separate, not unified. Then their tendency to not see what is so, but to ignore it. And finally, their tendency to not tell the truth to everyone about everything.

Then they would *drop* their tendency, described in Item 3, to say one thing and do another, and could get on with implementing "what works," having seen and told the whole truth about "what is so."

Wonderfully put. Wonderfully summarized. You're really stringing all of this together.

Thanks to the clarity with which it's being articulated here, yes. So I really don't need Item #4 explained any further. I get that HEBs from the Other Dimension see and say what is "so," and because they're hiding nothing and hiding *from* nothing, they do only what works to move forward their unified and identical agenda.

Humans will do the same thing when the species is fully awakened. It can also be one of their stepping stones for getting there.

I am so glad to hear that. That gives me hope—assuming that this awakening is really going to happen.

> You can be among those to help make it happen. That's what the Third Invitation is all about. And now humanity has the tools with which to create this awakening.
>
> And the Will.
>
> Now you have nearly instant worldwide communication, and a continually increasing portion of the total population that is self-selecting in their commitment to the process.
>
> As you put it earlier, you're just One Decision Away.

18

Okay, on to items #5, #6, and #7 then.

These all relate to parts of the human cultural story that are fairly deeply engrained in our societies everywhere on Earth.

> Okay. Let's recap them.
>
> Item #5 says: An awakened species does not embrace a principle in its civilization that correlates with the concepts that humans refer to as "justice" and "punishment."
>
> Item #6 says: An awakened species does not embrace a principle in its civilization that correlates with the concept that humans refer to as "insufficiency"
>
> Item #7 says: An awakened species does not embrace a principle in its civilization that correlates with the concept that humans refer to as "ownership."

Those are sweeping statements. How does any collective—even if it is a gathering or grouping of Highly Evolved Beings from Another Dimension—live without some code of conduct that regulates its behavior? And how do the members of such a collective live without ever experiencing that there is "not enough," especially if they never have anything they can call their own?

Let's look at the second part of that question first.

There is always "enough" of anything you think you need to survive when you know that you can't *not* survive.

In other words, when survival isn't the question, the idea of sufficiency or insufficiency ceases to have any significant meaning. The most important question in anyone's experience then is not *whether* they survive, but how.

Guaranteed eternal existence results in sharing completely and fully all that exists with all *who* exist, and the mutual conserving of any element or item that might be in less than endless supply in any particular setting, situation, or circumstance in the Realm of the Physical.

The result of this is that insufficiency is unheard of, as whatever in the physical environment may not be in endless supply is either easily done without, or substituted for with the creation of an equally useful and beneficial replacement.

It's nice that there are places in the universe where nothing essential ever runs out, but here on Earth we're not that lucky.

Actually, you are. There is no essential element that you need that you should run out of on your planet.

Really? What about something as simple as water? As I mentioned earlier, a huge percentage of humans to this very day has no access to clean water.

That is not a problem of lack of water, but lack of will. There are not enough people among your species who care about making clean water available to those who have no immediate access to it. If there were, this would not be a problem.

You're right, of course. The World Resources Institute reports on its website that "armed with the right information, countries facing extremely high stress can implement management and conservation strategies to secure their water supplies."

Unfortunately, a country at the bottom of the economic scale may not have that capacity. So it would be up to the richer nations of the world to help make this happen.

Yes, it's simply a matter of a civilization sharing. I assure you, there needs to be no place on Earth where people cannot have access to clean, pure water—and whatever else is needed to "make life work"—if the people of Earth simply cared enough about each other.

But it must be remembered that, as you pointed out earlier, we are talking about a species which lets over 650 of its own children die of starvation every hour.

Yes, we are a primitive species, for sure. Our actions—or lack of actions—demonstrate that.

Primitive or not, Earth's people shouldn't die from insufficient *food*, for goodness sake. Of all things, on a planet where you will scrape off enough food from the plates of diners tonight in restaurants from Paris to Los Angeles to Tokyo than would be needed to feed a small village in some areas of your world for a week, no child needs to starve to death.

I know. The U.S. Department of Agriculture estimates food waste in the United States alone to be about 30 to 40 percent of the food supply. An estimated 133 billion pounds of food from stores, restaurants and homes was wasted in 2010, according to official government statistics.

We are talking here about situations that would never, ever occur in the civilization of Highly Evolved Beings.

And that's the answer to your question about how it would be possible for there to *never* be "not enough" experienced by beings from Other Dimensions. There is always "enough" for a species that shares.

As for wondering how HEBs can co-exist without a "code of conduct that regulates their behavior," it is clear that the degree to which a species is living in an awakened state is reflected by the degree to which that species self-regulates.

The "code of conduct" of Highly Evolved Beings from the Other Dimension is elegantly simple: Do not have a thought regarding anyone, do not say a word regarding anyone, and do not do a thing regarding anyone that would you not want thought, said, or done regarding you.

Hmmm . . . here we go again. Seems like someone on Earth said that a very long time ago.

Actually, every religion on your planet teaches some version of what you've called the Golden Rule. The difference between human cultures and the civilizations of Highly Evolved Beings is that HEBs actually apply the law of reciprocity in their lives, rather than just giving it lip service.

Yes, but what happens in those civilizations if or when someone does do something to another that they would not like if it were done to them? What happens when someone commits—I'm sure you're going to tell me there is no such word in their language, but I'll say it here—a "crime"?

You're right, there is no such thing as "crime and punishment" in the culture of Highly Evolved Beings from the Other Dimension.

No one commits a "crime," because everyone understands that they are All One, and that an offense against another entity is an offense against the Self.

So there is no need for what you call "justice." The concept of "justice" is more deeply understood as what you would call Right Action.

In human society there is crime, of course. And justice is not always done in every case when a crime is committed. But the majority in our society at least tell themselves they can have the comfort of knowing that there will be justice in the hereafter. Judgment and everlasting punishment!

You're going to have to make up your mind here. Do you want an unconditionally loving God, or a judging, condemning, punishing God?

I know, I know. It's all very confusing. We're all very . . . complex. We don't want your judgments, but we do. We don't want your punishments, yet we feel lost without them. And when you say, as you've done consistently in every conversation we've ever had, "I will never punish you," we cannot believe that—and some of us almost become angry about it. Because if you're not going to judge and punish us, what will keep us walking the straight and narrow? And if there's no "justice" in heaven, who will undo all the injustice on Earth?

> Why are you counting on heaven to correct what you call "injustice"? Does not the refreshing, cleansing rain fall from the heavens?

Yes.

> And I tell you this: The rain falls on the just and the unjust alike.

But what about, "Vengeance is mine," sayeth the Lord?

> I never said that. One of you made that up, and the rest of you believed it.
> "Justice" is not something you experience *after* you act a certain way, but *because* you act a certain way. Justice is an *act*, not punishment *for* an act.
> An awakened species understands this.

I see that the problem with our society is that we seek "justice" *after* an "injustice" has occurred, rather than "doing justice" in every single case, through the choices and actions of every single human being, in the first place.

Right on the head! You've hit the nail right on the head! Justice is an action, not a *reaction*.

When everyone in our society acts justly, as every entity in an awakened species does, we will have no need for judgment and punishment as part of our civilization's constructions.

You will not.

But will such a thing ever be possible? Will there ever be a time when everyone acts justly?

There will, when everyone awakens.

Will everyone awaken?

You're deciding that now.

We have had parts of this present exchange in one of our previous conversations, in those exact words. Portions of what's just been said are a verbatim transcript of a back-and-forth exchange we've had before. I'm glad we've repeated it here, like a memorized passage from a wonderful play or a favorite poem.

I join in your being glad.

This present colloquy really is giving me a chance to synthesize much of what you've previously told me, combining it into a coherent whole.

It was intended to. Part of the Third Invitation is about full integration.

19

Well, that takes care of the concepts of insufficiency, justice and punishment mentioned in Items #5 and #6. Now what about Item #7 . . . "ownership"? Are we to own nothing?

> You may do whatever you wish, but in the civilizations of Highly Evolved Beings there is no such thing as ownership.

What is so bad about having something to call your own? Gee whiz, is every single thing we're doing on this planet wrong?

> There is no such thing as Right and Wrong. There is only What Works and What Does Not Work given—

—I know, I know . . . "given what it is you are trying to do."

> Yes. I keep repeating myself because you keep repeating yourself. You keep falling back on human

concepts that have no meaning in for an awakened species—like "right" and "wrong."

But what is so "non-functional" about having something we call our own? It seems to work just fine for most people.

You mean for most people who own most of the stuff.

Even most people who do *not* own most of the stuff *want* to own more.

Of course they do, because many of the people who do own most of the stuff are largely keeping it for themselves. The economic system you've put into place virtually guarantees that. There are exceptions, of course, but they are *exceptions*, not the rule.

Surely you see this.

You said yourself when we first began talking here that 85 of the world's richest people hold more wealth than 3.5 billion—half of your planet's population *combined*.

Yes, and of course I do see this. But I want to speak sometimes in this dialogue in the voice of James Thurber's "Everyman." Most people—all of these inequities aside—would not want to give up the idea of ever owning anything, of ever being able to call *anything* their own.

How do members of an awakened species do it?

They understand that since they are all One, every *thing* that exists belongs to every *one* that exists.

But how would that function as a practical matter? Everyone in our world can't till the soil and plant the seeds and harvest the crop and earn the income from every farm on the planet.

Every person cannot walk into every other person's dwelling as if it were their own and just hang out there. First of all, there wouldn't be a place big enough. And even if there were, could there be no privacy? Is everything to be shared, including husbands, wives, children, and all possessions of any kind?

How can that work?

In the civilization of an awakened species the idea of "ownership" is replaced by the concept of "stewardship."

Entities mutually agree on who shall have stewardship of what, who shall partner with whom, who shall raise offspring, and who shall perform what functions in the physical world.

No one "takes" anything or anyone that is being cared for by someone else through a stewardship or partnership agreement.

Those who create offspring do not imagine that they "own" their offspring, and those who partner with others do not imagine that they "own" their partners, and those who accept stewardship of anything else that is physical—be it land or some particular physical item—do not imagine that they "own" that item.

They are merely loving and caring for these other entities and these other items.

No one imagines, for instance, that because they are stewards of a particular parcel of the planet on which they have embodied, they "own" the minerals and water and whatever else is under that parcel, down to the center of the planet.

Nor does anyone imagine that they "own" the air, or the sky, *above* a particular parcel as high as the sky can go.

So there are no arguments about "how high is up" and "how far down is down" and who owns the "rights" to whatever is up or down there.

Such discussions would seem pointless and totally out of keeping among beings who understand that they are all One, and that no single entity or group of entities can possibly "own" a chunk of a planet—much less what's high above and far beneath it.

We have arguments between governments and individuals all the time over "air rights" and "water rights" and "mineral rights" on our planet.

Yes, you do. So where does "ownership" begin and end?

But if people didn't own *anything*, how could they make a profit from anything? And if they didn't make a profit, how could they earn a living?

Highly Evolved Beings have redefined the concept that you capture in your word, "profit." They do not consider it "profitable" if they benefit at the expense of another. They do not consider it acceptable if they win while another loses. And they especially do not consider it honorable if their winning *causes* another to lose. In their civilization, no one benefits unless everyone benefits.

It seems to be very difficult for most human beings to embrace such a notion. Which brings us to Item #8 on the list.

Item #8 says: An awakened species shares everything with everyone all the time. Humans in an unawakened state often do not, only sharing with others in limited circumstances.

To many people on this planet this seems to be simply impractical, unworkable.

Nonsense. You make it work all the time. You experience this right now in your own limited way. In your families, for instance.

You would never consider walking down the street in a rainstorm and holding an umbrella over your head alone, saying to your partner or your children: "Too bad you don't have an umbrella, too, but them's the breaks."

You would never think of eating all the apple pie by yourself without sharing with your partner or your children, saying: "Too bad there isn't enough here for all of us, but I'm sure going to enjoy mine."

I've used lighthearted examples, but you understand perfectly well the concept of refusing to profit or benefit if you are the only one who is profiting or benefiting, when it is your own family or loved ones who are suffering because you are not sharing.

The only difference between you and Highly Evolved Beings is that HEBs consider *everyone* to be their family and loved ones.

The solution to so many of Earth's problems is obvious.

Then why don't we embrace that solution? What stops us as a society from seeing the "obviousness" of that, and sharing everything with everyone?

The reason that you do not behave this way on Earth is that you do not think *there is enough* for everyone, and so you have to make sure that *you get yours.* It is the idea of scarcity that stifles the idea of full and complete sharing.

But there's more than enough for everyone! With food, water, energy, and nearly everything that we need to stay alive, we have a problem of distribution, not a problem of insufficiency.

That is largely true. You can share freely and lavishly all the gifts, talents, skills, knowledge, and abundance that life has given you, and watch life circulate back to you everything you require to stay alive.

You will surprise yourself with the knowing— and change your value system *because* of the know- ing—that you actually require much less than you may have thought to stay intact in a particular form as a body, and nothing at all to stay alive as a soul, given that staying alive is something you will always do, and cannot *not* do. It is merely a matter of what form your existence will take.

That is, of course, the question you answer with every choice, decision, and action in your entire life. What form shall my existence take?

What your planet could benefit from right now are a few more humans willing to demonstrate and model a new form that humanity could take, based on their belief in Sufficiency and Sharing, and in this way helping to awaken the species. These models will have to self-select, however, because no one is going to appoint or anoint them.

Hence, the Third Invitation.

But as I said earlier, how would we earn a living if everybody shared everything with everyone, and every definition of "profit" had to include benefit for everyone?

The experience of living is not something that one should have to "earn." Life is a gift, given to all of you, and it is not something you should have to make yourself *worthy of* every day of your existence.

A system could easily be devised by any civiliza- tion that would allow society to fulfill individual and group needs without the members of that society having to sell their soul and abandon their dreams in order to survive.

I hear that. There must be a way to create a social system in which everyone contributes more or less equal energy and everyone benefits more or less equally, with no one having to live a bare bones existence, and no one having to let go of any hope to do something they really love in this life in order to stay alive. Until our whole society changes, it's not going to be easy to create this, I guess.

Actually, your whole society *will* change when the majority sees how easy it really is for those of you who choose to lead the way. I said earlier that the object of self-selecting to help awaken the species was not to declare yourself to be a leader, but rather, one who has been led, by a deep inner knowing, to another way to be human.

Remember always that a "leader" is not one who says, "Follow me." A leader is one who says, "I'll go first."

You can't change overnight the way your Earthly societies function, but you can individually demonstrate and model the foundational qualities of an awakened species immediately—by going first.

20

This has been very helpful, and you know what? On reviewing Items 9-16 on our list, I think I pretty well understand most of those remaining.

Quickly summarize them for me then. Let's see. Here they are again:

#9: An awakened species creates a balance between technology and cosmology; between machines and nature. Humans in an unawakened state often do not.

#10: An awakened species would never under any circumstances terminate the current physical expression of another sentient being unless asked directly by that other being to do so. Humans in an unawakened state often kill other humans without that other human requesting them to.

#11: An awakened species would never do anything that could potentially damage or harm the physical environment which supports the members of the species when they are physicalized. Humans in an unawakened state often do so.

#12: An awakened species never poisons itself. Humans in an unawakened state often do so.

#13: An awakened species never competes. Humans in an unawakened state are often in competition with each other.

#14: An awakened species is clear that it needs nothing. Humans in an unawakened state often create a need-based experience.

#15: An awakened species experiences and expresses unconditional love for everyone. Humans in an unawakened state often cannot imagine even a Deity who does this, much less do they do it themselves.

#16: An awakened species has harnessed the power of metaphysics. Humans in an unawakened state often largely ignore it.

I'm clear that if we are to adopt the behaviors of an awakened species we'll have to bring our cosmology (our philosophies, beliefs, and understandings about the world and our decisions about who we are) up to speed with our technology (our weaponry, our genetic altering of crops, our cloning of mammals [and soon, humans], our life-extension medicine, and all the rest). If we don't, we'll be dealing with ethical, moral, and spiritual dilemmas that our old beliefs have left us not nearly ready to resolve.

I'm clear that if we were awakened we would stop damaging our environment at every turn . . . stop poisoning ourselves with the things we eat and drink and smoke and breathe and inject and listen to and watch . . . and stop our endless and often ruthless competitions for everything—money, power, fame, love, attention, sex, *everything*.

I'm clear that when we live as an awakened species we will transform what we've imagined to be our needs into preferences, and we will truly (and at last) love everyone without condition, even as we embrace and accept a God who does the same with us.

> You do understand. There is no need for me to
> go more deeply into any of this then.

The only two final items I feel the need to look at more closely are #10 and #16.

Item #10 says that members of an awakened species would never under any circumstances terminate the current physical expression of another sentient being without that other person requesting it. Humans kill other humans every minute of every day somewhere on their planet.

That last part can't be denied, but to be fair, much of the killing on Earth has been done in self-defense.

> All attack is called a defense in primitive cultures.
> Yet even as what you term "defense," a HEB would
> never terminate the physical expression of another
> sentient being without that being having asked it to
> do so.

We don't have a right to defend ourselves? Wow. That expectation is so high that no one on this planet could possibly buy into it. Even our religions and our laws tell us self-defense can justify killing. Are you saying that we do not have the right to protect ourselves if we have to kill another to do so?

You "have a right" to do anything you wish. What you are invited to remember is that every act is an act of self-definition. If you wish to define yourselves as a species that kills its own kind in order for some of its kind to survive, you may do so, and no one will stop you.

But the day may come when you will choose to stop yourself, if only out of seeing that in your frenzy to protect your species, you have nearly destroyed it.

But does this mean that when we are awakened, we will let anyone do anything to us, and not defend ourselves?

When your species awakens, it will not create scenarios in which its members *have* to defend themselves against each other.

When you awaken, you will lay down your arms—all of you, at once—and eschew forever the ways and the means of destroying each other. Your competitions for everything will end, and you will find ways to share everything that there is to share, including all the world's resources and all the amazing miracles of science, technology, and medicine that you have brought about.

For an awakened species, this will seem like a patently obvious and unquestionably appropriate thing to do.

You will have no reason to defend yourself, because no one will ever again have any reason to attack you—physically, emotionally, financially, or in any way whatsoever.

But what if we were attacked by some renegade individual who had not yet awakened? You know, that one-in-a-thousand or one-in-a-million person who is mentally unstable?

You would simply lay down your body and peacefully exit the Realm of the Physical, knowing that your "death" would not be an end to anything—except more violence.

Exactly as Obi Wan Kenobi did when threatened face-to-face by Darth Vader in one of those *Star Wars* movies.

Yes, exactly like that. Your science fiction depictions have more than once placed before humankind wonderfully illuminated ideas. That character in the movie did that, of course, because he knew he couldn't die; that the "villain" couldn't possible do anything to him that would terminate his existence.

But what if we were all attacked, all at once, by entities other than our own species? It was you who said earlier that there are advanced beings from other planets in the Realm of the Physical who are violent. Don't we have to worry about them coming to Earth one day and destroying us?

No. Violent sentient beings from other galaxies will not be allowed to destroy your civilization. The Highly Evolved Beings existing in Another Dimension would make that impossible.

Why? Why would they step in and do that?

Because it serves their purpose to express and experience their True Identity by doing so. They have understandings and objectives different from beings who experience themselves primarily as physical entities living in a physical dimension.

Yet they will let an entire civilization dismantle life as it has known it on its own planet. They are letting us do this right now.

That is an act of a civilization's conscious choice, of its Collective Will, it is not an act that violates the Collective Conscious Will of another civilization on another planet.

Even on Earth you make this difference. It is the difference between someone choosing to end their own life of their own free will, or someone choosing to end the life of another against that other's will.

On a galactic scale, the first would be compassionately allowed by HEBs, while the second would be stopped.

You once told me that no one dies at a time or in a way that is not of their choosing.

> That is correct.
>
> I said that in our last conversation—a dialogue that you turned into a book titled *Home with God in a Life That Never Ends.*
>
> I understand that this is one of the most difficult and challenging of the revelations you have been given, but this does not make it any less true.
>
> Life's mysteries are impossible to resolve within the limitations of the human mind and the incomplete data held by any just-emerging species.
>
> I can only assure you that at the level of soul, the events to which you refer are experienced as being in alignment with the spiritual agenda of the soul Itself.

Yet individuals are murdered—killed against their will—all the time on Earth, and from what you seem to be saying, on other planets where entities are violent as well.

> Individual Superconscious Will cannot and will not ever be violated in this regard. Thus, when you choose to do the thing that you call "die"—which you do at a Superconscious level (that is, the level of soul), not at a Conscious level (i.e., the level of Mind)—you will move from the physical to the metaphysical voluntarily. When you don't choose to do so, you will not.

21

I think that deserves and requires more explanation, a closer exploration. But I'd like to move now to Item #16 and come back to this later, because there seems to be something really important for us to look at in this final item from the list, and the two may bear some relationship to each other. Item #16 tells us that an awakened species has harnessed the power of metaphysics. Humans in an unawakened state often largely ignore it.

To what are we referring here?

> What is being said in this Item is that the scope and breadth of universal wisdom and creative metaphysical power is largely unused by humanity.

I'm going to ask you again here, as I have done before: Can you give me an example?

> Yes. You said yourself a little while ago that a man named Émile Coué proved the effectiveness of autosuggestion in the early part of the 20th century.

Well, he proved it to *his* satisfaction, anyway.

You don't believe his results?

Well, I believe them, yes. But not everyone might agree.

The question here is, since you, yourself, say you believe in this process, do you use it? Have you used it as a tool in dealing with your own physical ailments?

Well, not regularly, no.
Wait. I have to be truthful here.

That would be good.

I've never used it. I believe that the energetic power of the mind can affect the energetic signature of cells within the body—we've talked about this exact possibility—but no, I've never used the Coué method to address any of my physical ailments or conditions.

Case closed.

I guess our human society is not ready, on a grand scale, to grapple with metaphysics, to deal with what some have called alchemy, and to rigorously apply what so many have called the power of positive thinking.

Some individuals have done it, and some spiritual groups—relatively small as a proportion of the whole of humanity—have done it, but I'm seeing what you're saying now. As a civilization we have not come anywhere near harnessing the power of metaphysics.

No, the human race has not. It is, however, becoming more and more aware of it, and is moving, step by step, in that direction.

Yes. There was a movie and a book out a few years ago called *The Secret*, which talked all about the power that lies within us to create our own reality. And as an illustration of this, the movie showed a man finding the car of his dreams in the driveway, a woman suddenly noticing a diamond necklace adorning her bodice, and even a nine-year-old boy rejoicing over the shiny new bicycle just outside the back door.

But I can see that these are just our first baby steps. I couldn't help but wonder, if the "secret" was so powerful, why wasn't it being used to create, say, world peace?

This idea wasn't even mentioned in the movie as a possible application—pretty much letting us know where the members of our species place world peace vis-à-vis new cars, diamond necklaces, and shiny new bikes on the scale of importance. Or at least, where the movie's producers assumed we place it.

You could, of course, create world peace using basic metaphysics.

Yes, my wonderful friend John Hagelin has traveled the globe making this point. A renowned quantum physicist, science and public policy expert, educator, and author, Dr. Hagelin offers us this from his online writings:

"Most people don't know how deeply their own consciousness is connected to the collective fate of the planet—or how they can use a powerful, scientifically tested technology of consciousness to help *create* world peace on Earth virtually overnight.

"More than fifty demonstration projects and twenty-three studies published in leading peer-reviewed journals have shown that this new consciousness-based approach to world peace neutralizes the ethnic, political, and religious tensions in society that give rise to crime, violence, terrorism, and war.

"The approach has been tested on the local, state, national, and international levels, and it has worked every time, resulting in highly significant drops in negative social trends and improvements in positive trends.

"Large groups of peace-creating experts, practicing these technologies of consciousness together, dive deep within themselves to the most fundamental level of mind and matter, which physics calls the unified field.

"From that level of life they create a tidal wave of harmony and coherence that can permanently alter society for the better, as the research confirms. And this consciousness-based approach is holistic, easy to implement, non-invasive, and cost effective."

(See *www.PermanentPeace.org* for more information.)

So the question is, what would it take for us to use this . . . can I call it, *"spiritual technology?"*

What do you think?

Nothing more than an awakening. Even just a beginning awareness of these things could get things started on a larger scale. I was struck by one of the video programs that John Hagelin made about all this, which ends with this quote:

"There is far more evidence that group meditation can turn off war like a light switch than there is evidence that aspirin reduces headache pain."

There you have it. Tell everyone you know. And have them tell everyone they know. Metaphysics works. It's the lynchpin of the universe. And Highly Evolved Beings know this.

22

Okay, thank you. That completes the overview on that list, and I found it be to very instructive. I do think, as I said, that our exploration of Item #10, and some of the observations about death there, deserve some expansion.

> Item #10 again: An awakened species would never under any circumstances terminate the current physical expression of another sentient being unless asked directly by that other being to do so. Humans in an unawakened state often kill other humans without that other human requesting them to.

This is not a subject that I feel we can go over lightly. And I understand now how, if we can much better use the power of metaphysics to deal with illnesses and other events, this could have a relationship to my death. But were you telling me that if I am murdered, or killed in an accident by a reckless driver, or whatever—that I have died because I chose to?

Why would any soul choose to die?

> The answer is as varied as there are souls in the universe. But you can be assured that each death

serves the purpose of every soul in that moment, or
it would not occur.

What about those of us left behind, mourning the
loss? Did they take that into account?

> They surely did. They have taken *everything* into
> account. And they do their very best to ease your
> pain of loss by helping you understand, and *experi-
> ence*, that they have actually not died, but simply
> celebrated their Continuation Day.

What do you mean, "experience?" We can experience
that they are still alive?

> Many people already know what I mean, if any-
> one close has celebrated their Continuation Day.
> Vast anecdotal evidence reveals that those who
> have "passed on" have found ways to make it clear
> to their surviving loved ones that they are "still alive."

Gosh, this dialogue is getting more and more "out there."

> Actually, it's getting more and more "in there."
> It's moving more and more into what you already
> know, deep within, but just may not have been able
> to fully or openly embrace, given the current Cul-
> tural Story of your very young species.

Putting this all together then, I guess it wouldn't *matter* if aliens from other planets attacked us. If we didn't
choose to "die," we wouldn't and *couldn't*.

No. You would create a manner and a means by which that would not be possible. Such as, for instance, something or someone intervening.

Ah, I see. The intervention of HEBs, for instance.

For instance. And this energy signature of what the soul chooses, or what you would call the Superconscious Will, works for you individually as well.

If, as an individual, you have not chosen at a Superconscious level to leave your physical form, you will not, even in the most treacherous or life-threatening circumstances. You may have what others will call a "near miss" or a "miraculous recovery" or an "incredible escape," but you will not die.

The Collective Superconscious Will—that is, the demonstrated will of everyone in the Collective—is the single and only influence affecting the embodying or disembodying of the Collective, and the individual Superconscious Will is the single and only influence affecting the embodying or disembodying of Individuals. This is how the energy of Life works.

It is the demonstrated Collective Superconscious Will that it does not choose for the Collective to be annihilated *en masse*, or destroyed as a civilization.

I hate to argue with you here, but whole groups of people have died on this planet, and it has happened more than once. Are you saying that it's *perfectly okay* that this has happened, because everyone wanted to die?

I am not saying that it is "okay that it happened" the way or at the time that it did. The choice to experience any event as "okay" or "not okay" is a choice for every person who is affected in any way by any event to make. I will never tell a person that their choice is "right" or "wrong." Their choice is their choice, and it is not for me to judge.

You don't judge anything, actually, do you?

No. I know that in human terms there may be many things that would understandably be defined by humans as "not okay"—and to call them anything else might even be considered unhealthy and cruel within the context of normal and appropriate human behavior. It is by this device that you establish the fundamental values of your civilization— even if you do not all live by them.

But I don't make those assessments or evaluations, because to do so would be to rob you of your freedom to create your own reality.

What I am saying here is that no human being's experience of what your species calls "death" can occur in violation of that person's individual Superconscious Will. And no civilization's experience of what your species calls total destruction can occur in violation of that civilization's Collective Superconscious Will.

You made this point now repeatedly. But—again, not to be argumentative, but—doesn't saying such a thing give permission, in a sense, to those who would go on a rampage and kill others—individually, or God help us, *en masse*—to serve their own twisted purpose?

No, it gives comfort to those who would see others as having been victimized in such a situation. It allows those who have been left behind to find the peace of healing, knowing that their loved one is celebrating their Continuation Day—and has done so with full awareness of the choice they have made, and even with full understanding and compassion for those who collaborated in their departure.

As well, it may even actually stop someone who may feel no guilt about planning such a rampage, and then becomes aware of the information here, because it could rob the potential perpetrator of the satisfaction of doing what they think is damaging to another, dissolving much of what might have been their motivation.

I would never have thought of that.

And there is this: Persons who would go ahead and kill others anyway, individually or in a group, do not seek or need permission from something or someone outside of themselves to do so. They will have justified their actions on a basis entirely different from anything said here.

Yes, but what they read here could help them feel okay about it.

> They already feel okay about it, or they wouldn't
> have done it.

You know, I can see how what's been said here might not fit into the overall understanding of many. I mean, what's been laid out here probably isn't going to mesh for the majority of people.

> So long as anyone experiences reality as a vic-
> tim/villain scenario, it will not. But there are no
> victims and no villains in the world. Or anywhere in
> the universe. There are only sentient beings physi-
> cally and metaphysically evolving, and helping each
> other evolve.
>
> It is as I have said to you previously: I have sent
> you nothing but angels.
>
> If you felt that you would significantly shorten
> the evolutionary process of an entire species—that
> is, of *billions*—by allowing your Self to exit your
> physical body at a certain time in a certain way,
> would you do it?
>
> Don't think about your answer at the level of
> mind. Think about it at the level of soul.

When I think about it at the level of soul, I realize that my existence cannot be threatened and my life cannot and will not end. So to simply change the form of my existence from the physical to the metaphysical—espe-cially knowing that I can change it back again whenever I wish—knowing that billions would move forward in their evolutionary process because of it, makes it a very easy decision.

I would see it as what I called, earlier, a "Burning Building Moment," when you rush in to save the baby and your own physical survival is not even part of your thought process; not part of the equation. I would make whatever choice brings the greatest benefit to the largest number of my fellow sentient beings.

> Of course you would, because that's Who You Are.
>
> I want to tell you again that Love is who you all are.
>
> It is because of this that you would actually forgive the person or group appearing to be the cause of your death, because you would realize that at a conscious level they did not even know what they were doing.
>
> Then, when you moved to total awareness in the Realm of Pure Being (if it does not happen before), you would abandon any need to forgive them, because forgiveness would be replaced with understanding. You would comprehend completely how a sentient being could or would do such a thing.

You have told me in the past that understanding replaces forgiveness in the mind of the master.

> And so it does.
>
> All of these things would be experienced by you precisely *because* you are made up of the energy you call Love, personified and magnified in the free-will choices and decisions that you make, the understandings that you embrace, and the expressions of Self that you place into the ongoing and simultaneous creation within the Ultimate Reality.

You do not have to wait until you find yourself in the Realm of Pure Being. This awareness may be embraced by you at any time. The continued expansion of your awareness is what evolution is all about.

23

In the book *When Everything Changes, Change Everything*, there was mention of "the Realm of Pure Being." Is this what you have been referring to here?

It is, indeed.

Yes, I remember now. The Realm of Pure Being was said to be one of three aspects of the Kingdom of God. The other two were the Realm of the Spiritual and the Realm of the Physical.

Have I not told you that in my kingdom there are many mansions?

You have. You have said so explicitly. And you are saying now that even Earth is part of the Kingdom of Heaven?

Not "even" Earth, but the entire Realm of the Physical is part of the kingdom.

As I noted earlier, Highly Evolved Beings are able to move easily and effortlessly between being embodied or not embodied in their dimension—and they do spend time in the Realm of the Physical, which is in your dimension, when it serves their purpose.

As we also noted earlier, you do the same, moving effortlessly, too, between realms. But when you spend more than just a brief time in a metaphysical state, you call your movements "lifetimes."

Can humans move into a metaphysical state when we are *not* between lifetimes?

You can, and do. You do it in certain kinds of what you call "dreams." You do it in what you have termed "out-of-body" experiences. You do it in what we have already described here as "near-death encounters." There are those of you who have been known to do it in meditation. And some whom you have called the masters among you—both now and through the ages—have embodied and disembodied and embodied again during what you define as a single lifetime.

So during a particular journey through a particular "life," you can and do experience being metaphysical. But this is not a usual or everyday experience for you.

That's why you keep using that specific combination of words—"beings living primarily in the Physical Realm"—to describe humans.

And other entities, whom you have called "beings from outer space," who exist on other planets in the Realm of the Physical.

Thank you. I understand your use of the term clearly now. One last thing, then, in this whole thought stream. You've used another interesting term—"Superconscious Will"—several times in this dialogue. Can you explain that usage?

Yes. As I shared in detail in the conversation that became your book *Friendship with God*, all sentient beings experience consciousness at four levels: The Subconscious, the Conscious, the Superconscious, and the Supraconscious.

Energies of creation are emitted by every entity from one of these four levels.

Given that yours is a very young species, many human beings act without full awareness of how they are doing what they are doing. They produce their creations (and thus, their experience) from a particular level of consciousness from which they are viewing life and making decisions, but they may not be doing so with full awareness of, or absolute intention regarding, which level they are operating from.

It would sure help for me to have an illustration of this, because you lost me around that last turn.

Well then, here are some classic examples:

One I offered earlier is of a person healing a wound. That person is creating from the Subconscious level—sending, for example, white blood cells to the site of a small cut—and that person most often has come from this level of consciousness without even thinking about it. They may or may not have a full awareness of what they are doing and how they are creating.

A person rushing to the airport is creating from the Conscious level, and that person most often has come from this level of consciousness *because* they are thinking about it. They usually have a full awareness of what they are doing and how they are creating.

A person pushing someone out of the way of an oncoming bus and risking their life in doing it is creating from the Superconscious level, and that person has come from this level of consciousness *after* thinking about it—but putting the data together so rapidly that it *appears* they did *not* think about it. They always have a full awareness of what they are doing and how they are creating.

A person choosing to awaken themselves and their species by being a demonstration and a model of their True Identity is creating from the Supraconscious level, and that person has come from that level of consciousness intentionally, with total awareness of what they are doing and how they are creating.

Sentient beings are demonstrating absolute, complete, and full awareness of Who They Are and How Life Works when they deliberately and intentionally choose, *ahead of time*, a particular State of Consciousness from which to express and experience any thought, word, or action.

Sentient beings are demonstrating a lower level of Awareness when they express and experience a thought, word, or action from a State of Consciousness they have not deliberately and intentionally selected.

Many sentient beings vacillate between levels of awareness, thus altering significantly the quality and effectiveness of their thoughts, words, and actions across the moments of their life.

Masters are beings who do not vacillate between levels of Awareness, but consistently select, with deliberateness and clear intention, the State of Consciousness from which they wish their thoughts, words, and actions to emerge.

You couldn't have put all this any better. I understand it perfectly.

Excellent.

What I *don't* understand is how to reach a level of mastery; how to stop the endless vacillation of my awareness.

That's what you've come to me for.

You can show me how?

I can and I have been, all along. You may not have been paying close attention. Now you are. You're awakening to the fact that you're awake already. This is not a small thing. This is the beginning of the beginning, so to speak.

Now watch your awareness expand in the days just ahead. You'll feel this expansion, even as you continue experiencing and remembering this dialogue.

Now I understand why Highly Evolved Beings from the Other Dimension will not allow us to be destroyed by any attack from other beings in the Realm of the Physical. HEBs always act in accordance with the Collective Superconscious Will of the civilizations whose members experience themselves as primarily physical beings.

That is correct. You do now understand.

And so we're protected on Earth from the violence of an interstellar species.

You are safe from all but one.

Omigosh, which one?

Earthlings. You are not yet safe from yourself.

24

That was cute. That was very cute.

I wasn't being cute. I was being accurate.

But is it not the Collective Superconscious Will of humanity not to be destroyed?

It is.

Then how can humanity be a threat to itself?

Humanity cannot and will not be threatened as a Collective. It will always exist, because it is the Superconscious Collective Will of humanity to do so. The question is not *whether* the Collective called "humanity" will exist, but *how* it will exist. What shall be the quality of the life of human beings?

You are deciding that now—right now—on your planet. Much will depend on whether the largest number of you awaken.

Those of you who self-identify as having accepted the Third Invitation can and will play a major role in the outcome that is produced on your planet.

All that you've just said opens up so many areas for further discussion. I don't know exactly how to continue here—and I really don't want to get too far afield with this dialogue. I want it to be *relevant.*

You can't be "too far afield" or "irrelevant" no matter what you ask. All the topics are the same topic, looked at from different angles.

The topic is . . .

LIFE:
What is true about it,
and how you can live
that truth.

Okay, then I'll just roll on here. Because this relates to me, as I am living my human life, and to all of us who have found ourselves following this conversation, and who may choose to self-select to do what might be done to assist in the awakening of the species.

Good.

You've described how Highly Evolved Beings from Another Dimension move from the physical to the meta-physical and back again at will. Then you've said that we do the same.

That's correct.

Well, not many human beings experience that they do the same. We're born—or as you put it, we "embody"—

when we do. We don't experience having any control over that. And we die when we die. We have no control over that, either.

That would be *incorrect*.

Okay, it's true that some people die by their own hands, so they did exert control over when they died, but they certainly had no control over when they were born.

You will continue to imagine that all of this is true about both what you call your "birth" and your "death" so long as you think of yourself as a body.

You have told me before, actually, that I am not a body. You have said that I *have* a body, but that Who I Am is not a body.

I am happy that you have remembered this. It is the most important single piece of information you could ever receive about your Self, and that you could ever share with anyone.

Each entity in the Other Dimension thinks of itself as an emanation of the Essential Essence. Or, using the word that we've employed so far throughout this dialogue, and one that you may be able to relate to better: a soul.

And so you see that you are not "far afield" in exploring this. In fact, this is central to the larger discussion about what it would look like for humans to model their life on the lives of Highly Evolved Beings.

So use what we're looking at now to create a larger context for what's already been shared here about the possibilities for humanity's tomorrow.

Perfect. All right. I can see the connection. You want me to understand that it is because they know themselves to be what we call "souls" that Highly Evolved Beings from Another Dimension experience that they can embody at will, that they never die, that their purpose and only desire is to express and experience Divinity, that there is nothing they need, nothing they own, nothing over which they have stewardship that they will not share, nothing they will not do for those they love—and no one they do not love.

What a wonderful summary. You've really pulled this all together now. Good for you.

And good for all of those who will self-select as helpers in choosing to do whatever they may be able to do to help themselves and to help others in the awakening process.

Yes.

I know that the more I can understand about being a soul with a body and not a body with a soul, the more I can live the life that all sentient beings are invited to live, by simply knowing and embracing their True Identity.

Now it's all very well and good to explore a list of differences between an awakened species which fully accepts its True Identity and humans, but I can see how people could have a difficult time accepting any of what's being explored here (and this is important, by the way, if I and others are to awaken the species) if no more information is offered about these HEBs, as we have been calling them; who they are and how they are helping us.

You said that they sometimes take physical form outside of their own dimension, in order to help species throughout the Realm of the Physical.

That's correct.

So if and when Highly Evolved Beings take a physical form when not in their dimension, how do they avoid being noticed?

Sometimes they are noticed—and want to be. They may take on a form that is normal for them in their own dimension, but very much not normal in the environment they are visiting, thereby *allowing* themselves to be noticed. They would do this if their intention is to let those living outside of their dimension know that (a) they exist, (b) they are present, and (c) they mean no harm, and have only come to help.

If a Highly Evolved Being feels that being seen in its own physical form would shock or dismay and rally unnecessary defenses, thereby working against its very reason for moving from the metaphysical to the physical in a location outside of its dimension in the first place (which is to help, not frighten), it will take on the form of the beings it seeks to assist, and will do so in a way that allows it to meld into another civilization without making its presence disruptive, dismaying, disturbing, startling, or alarming in any way.

How will it accomplish that?

It will embody at the earliest possible moment in the life cycle of the beings it seeks to help, moving through the same developmental passage of every entity in that civilization.

Ah, I get it! In this way a HEB don't just suddenly "show up" somewhere, having to explain itself at every turn to every native of the local civilization.

Exactly. By taking on the form of a newly born or newly emergent native of the host planet, a complete history and record of the HEB's presence in the local population is created. Hence, there is no disruption generated by its arrival in a civilization's environment.

And there is a second, no less important, reason for emerging in a civilization at the onset of the life cycle of all native entities in that civilization. The HEB is assured that it understands the local history and habits, beliefs and behaviors thoroughly and *experientially*.

So as far as anyone in that host environment is concerned, the HEB is just "one of the gang." It doesn't "stand out" because of any physical difference; it doesn't "scare the locals."

That is correct.

Okay, so here comes the Big Question: Are you saying that a member of this awakened species, if it seeks to help us, can take on human form?

> It can, indeed. Highly Evolved Beings have the ability to do so.

Have they done so? Just tell it to me straight. *Have they?*

> Yes. On rare occasion, yes.

So it's *true* that there are—to co-opt a popular phrase—"aliens among us." Not just aliens in the universe, but aliens among *us.*

> Not in the sense that I know you mean, no.
>
> You shouldn't get the impression that thousands, hundreds, or even dozens of sentient beings from another dimension are walking the streets and sitting next to you in restaurants, or standing alongside you in supermarket checkout lines. In that sense, there are not, and have not been, aliens "among you."

Well, what are you saying, then?

> I'm saying that on rare occasion across human history there has been a time when a Highly Evolved Being has taken human form as a means of physically delivering—and, more important, visibly mod-

eling—a particular message that could have been lost in the maelstrom of human affairs had it not been placed before your species for its consideration in the most direct way.

This may happen, on your time scale, once in a thousand years or more. It has been an infrequent and isolated occurrence.

The far more usual method of seeking to assist the civilization on Earth (or any planet) is through the gentle sending of healing and supportive energy, in the form of comfort, insights, concepts, and ideas for humanity to consider living by. This is done through a process of what you might call inspiration.

No being or entity energetically enters anyone's mind in a personally intrusive way—that would break an unwritten code or guideline surrounding the process, which does not allow any entity to violate the private space of any sentient being's thoughts. HEBs simply place ideas into the space of life, and these ideas resonate with beings in the physical realm who are projecting a similar energetic signature. It is energetic resonance that draws those ideas to them. They will then often actually say, "I just 'got' an idea." And they *did*. That is exactly what happened, and a perfect way to describe it.

So if they don't ever energetically enter a human being's mind, how exactly *do* HEBs get their ideas and suggestions noticed, much less listened to or embraced?

By simply dropping them into the slipstream of what your Carl Jung called the Collective Unconscious. Humans who resonate with these ideas then find themselves magnetized by their vibrational match.

Everything, of course, is energy, vibrating at a particular frequency. Every sentient being in the universe is attracted to vibrational energy matches. It is by this means that sentient beings find themselves inspired.

Now by far the largest number of ideas come to humans from their own observations and inventiveness, so the concepts and insights of HEBs represent only a small percentage of these. Those concepts and insights are in the energy flow, however, and have been known to come to the conscious awareness of persons who find an attraction to them. Often these are humans who've placed themselves in certain idea-oriented occupations.

The result: far reaching, uplifting, and what have been called revolutionary ideas frequently show up in books, films, television programs, videos, magazines, newspapers, select social media, and other avenues that extend to the masses.

I can see that happening on a regular basis. I don't know exactly which ideas are coming from where, but I have certainly seen a lot of movies, books, online articles, and other messages dealing with a better way for humans to interact, offering elements of a wonderfully altered cultural story for our species, and presenting daring new scenarios for improving our collective future.

Now you've got me wondering. Is this very experience that I am having right now part of that process? Have all of my conversations with God actually been conversations with Highly Evolved Beings?

No. This conversation is not being sourced by the Highly Evolved Beings to which I have been referring, if that's what you're asking. It is part of the larger process through which Divinity is being expressed across the cosmos.

Every sentient being in the universe has the ability to communicate directly with The Divine. It is not, and never has been, necessary to go through any intermediary, a Highly Evolved Being or anyone else.

All human beings are having conversations with me all the time. They are simply not "announcing" it, or they are calling it something else, usually for fear of being ridiculed or marginalized.

Highly Evolved Beings are simply more *aware* of their eternal connection with Original Source, would never deny that they are expressions of It, experience that they are in constant communication with the Essential Essence that you call God, and find both joy and fulfillment in passing on what they have come to understand and experience as a result of their eternal connection and continual unity with me.

And so it has been that a Highly Evolved Being has come to Earth on occasion through the millennia.

Yes, when doing so would offer the very best chance for a message that would be of great benefit to the advancement of your species to be delivered and modeled in such a way that it could not be missed.

The message does not have to be accepted, mind you. Nothing is ever required of, or forced on, anyone by a Highly Evolved Being. But delivering and modeling the message in a way that can't be missed is in every case a HEB's objective.

25

I would very much like to understand all of this even better. You may think that I have an unquenchable thirst for details, but I find it hard to accept what I can't hold in my mind as comprehensively as possible.

Please don't worry. I have invited you before, in previous conversations, to set aside any feelings that you should explain yourself, or apologize.

Yes, you have, thank you.

Just be sure, because of the fascination of it, not to make this continuing dialogue so much about the technical details of Highly Evolved Beings that you lose sight of the most important aspect of all that you're being invited to live and to share—which is how all of you can elevate your experience on Earth to that of an awakened species called Humanity.

You will want to make sure that we talk about how you can fully integrate wonderfully elevated ideas into your daily life, changing your own behaviors in the process.

And we want to talk more about love. True love.
Real love. The foundational energy of the universe.
And how you can experience and express that in its
purest form.

Thank you, I won't lose that focus. I do want to bring
all of this back to topics of huge importance and relevance
to my own personal experience. And it is, in fact, because
I know that it *is* of personal relevance that I've accepted
without pause the Third Invitation. I realize that this is
going to do *me* more good than anyone else.

But I am, of course, fascinated with what you've been
telling me since you said that those of us who choose to do
so don't have to worry about undertaking the mission of
awakening the species all alone—that we have help.

You do.

And that this help is coming from Highly Evolved
Beings from Another Dimension.

It is.

So there's no way I'm not going to want to know all
that I can know about that. I'm assuming that how they
are trying to help us has been by sharing some of the
actions, choices, and decisions that humans might take
as we become more fully awakened, so I am so grateful to
have reviewed that list and explored some of its implications for humanity.

But my mind is signaling me that before I can even
begin to fully absorb that kind of information, it needs

to deal with some very real skepticism about whether any so-called Highly Evolved Beings have actually visited us . . . and if so, how they could have "gotten away with it" without discombobulating the entire world.

If I could get a handle on that, I'm guessing I could get my logical mind out of the way enough to explore how human society could change if we lived as an awakened species.

What do you need to know, then, about all this?

I'd first like to see if I clearly understand what I've been told so far.

Ask any question you wish.

Thank you.

On those occasions when a Highly Evolved Being has physicalized on Earth—and you said it has been very rare, but that it has happened—you explained that it would not just "drop in" as a human being suddenly showing up, walking around as a fully developed person, but would embody at the beginning of the human life cycle, is that correct?

That is what is so, yes.

So I have to ask . . . this is with the awareness of the mother and father of this baby—do I have this right? If this truly is a Highly Evolved Being, I can't imagine that it would embody in any way invasively or intrusively.

You are correct. Both humans begetting this offspring would be gently and lovingly imbued with a
deep inner awareness that they have an opportunity to create a child with a very special purpose,
and the option is theirs to do so or not.

But you know, even with that having been said, the idea
of a couple giving birth to an alien being feels very difficult
for me to accept. I'm feeling very challenged by this.

The Highly Evolved Being who became the offspring of humans was not "alien" in any way, any
more than you will be "alien" when you leave your
physical body through the process you call "death,"
then return from the metaphysical for another life
in the physical through the process you call "birth."
A Highly Evolved Being is simply a fully awakened entity who has moved through the same cycle
and is doing the same thing, with the difference
that such a being has moved from the metaphysical
to the physical inter-dimensionally. On rare occasion, one has taken on physicality in the form called
"human."

I see.

Nor would you be an "alien" in any other form
in the physical universe that you might choose to
assume. You would be "one of them" in any civilization in the Realm of the Physical in which you may
decide to take physical form.

I'm sorry? You just lost me again.

You may choose to physicalize in any form that you choose, anywhere in the universe. Did you know that?

No, I did not know that. I probably ran across that idea somewhere, in some reading I've done or some story I've heard, but it did not know it was true.

It is.

Are you saying I can choose to reincarnate somewhere else other than on Earth?

You have that option, yes.

Why would I do that?

As part of your soul's journey, as part of its mission to experience every aspect of itself that it knows itself to be.
For the very same reason, your soul may have left other civilizations to embody on Earth.

Are you telling me that *I* might be an alien *here?*

No. You would no more be an 'alien', having been born here, than a Highly Evolved Being who came to Earth would be. That is the point. You would simply have come here to experience every aspect of life that existence on Earth can provide, while a Highly

Evolved Being from Another Dimension would have
come here to assist you.

Have I ever actually done any of this? I know you're
saying that it is possible for a soul to do so, but has my particular soul ever incarnated somewhere else in the cosmos?

Let me ask you a question. Have you ever gazed
up at the night sky and felt as if you were looking
homeward?

Yes, actually, I have. That's an interesting question
you've asked, and I have to admit, I've actually felt *home-
sick* sometimes, with my attention drawn like a magnet to
a particular sector.

Do you think you would feel that way about
somewhere you've never been?

My goodness, this conversation is taking me to a
whole slew of unexpected places.

If you want the expected, you probably should
not be having a conversation with God.

No, probably not.
So you're saying that souls have their choice, between
lifetimes, of where to become physical.

The whole experience of all souls is about
choice. Always and forever, choice, choice, choice.

Free choice. The choice of Divine Beings, being Divine.

Oh, man . . . this is so . . . I don't know . . . *incredible* is the word my mind comes up with. I'm fighting not to say, "impossible to believe."

Why are you so amazed? Is it not written: *Ye are Gods—?*

Yes, yes, but who believes that stuff? Who takes it *literally?*

What was the point of the message if you were going to toss it aside?

I'm hearing that. But there's so much in so many holy scriptures, and not every word of it is true. Let's be fair. There have been some misinterpretations, some misunderstandings of the original . . . shall I say . . . "revelations." So we have to pick and choose, and it is not easy knowing which to hold close and deeply believe.

Yes, that's why, once in every great while, a Highly Evolved Being from Another Dimension will embody in human form to deliver and *model*, in human form, the grandest truths, making it more possible for your emerging species to sort this all out.

When a Highly Evolved Being becomes human in form, it will absorb, embrace, and embody all aspects of humanness, down to the smallest detail and cellular characteristic. It is, therefore, not alien, but entirely human, yet with characteristics of

thought and temperament, awareness and understanding that its knowing and experience brings it.

And so this soul could really be called a highly evolved
human.

That is exactly so. HEBs, like you, are souls—
manifesting Divinity in physical form. They are souls
who have chosen to move from the metaphysical
to the physical in your dimension in order that they
may have the experience of their Divinity by assisting other souls in remembering their own.

That is a wonderful clarification, a perfect exegesis.

26

And so, a Highly Evolved Being lives through the developmental years like every other member of our species, then begins to do the work of helping the species awaken when it grows into adulthood.

Sometimes even before then.

It begins helping when it is a child?

Sometimes, yes.

How does it not stand out?

Actually, it does. It is almost always called a "stand out." And it may have surprised others with what it seemed to know and with what it said. But the HEB's only objective was to leave information here in a way that articulated higher ideals for the consideration of a still developing culture.

How did a Highly Evolved Being do that? How did it "leave" this information? Tell me how we were helped when a HEB came to Earth.

The HEB spoke to people—sometimes its elders, later in life its peers—and offered things that perked up ears and that have been remembered, in some cases for centuries.

It also modeled, by its behavior, how an awakened species could live. This was its most significant contribution to the culture, its chief means of message delivery.

Some Highly Evolved Beings left writings, adding ideas to the culture in many forms, from novels to poetry to dramatized entertainments, in which they placed enormous truths.

Such as? I'm ready to start hearing about how an awakened species thinks. I'm hoping for examples now.

Here are some: Eliminate the concept of ever being offended—much less seeking revenge. Offer only high blessings to one who hurts you. Do away with defense of any kind.

Well, those really are pretty . . . how to put this . . . "advanced" ideas. Any human being saying such things would probably be written off as standing way outside the mainstream, and not taken very seriously.

Don't be too sure. Such ideas have been placed into your culture and have *not* been written off, but actually honored.

It was the man called Buddha who told his monks that even if bandits on a road attacked and robbed them, "Whoever of you harbors ill will at heart would not be upholding my teaching. Monks, even in such a situation you should train yourselves thus: 'Neither shall our minds be affected by this, nor for this matter shall we give vent to evil words, but we shall remain full of concern and pity, with a mind of love, and we shall not give in to hatred.

"'On the contrary, we shall live projecting thoughts of universal love to those very persons, making them as well as the whole world the object of our thoughts of universal love—thoughts that have grown great, exalted, and measureless. We shall dwell radiating these thoughts which are void of hostility and ill will.' It is in this way, monks, that you should train yourselves."

And wasn't it a man named Jesus who said: "Love your enemies, bless them that curse you, do good to them that hate you, and pray for them which despitefully use you, and persecute you"—? And did he not also say, "If a man slaps you on the right cheek, turn and offer him your left"—?

Are you saying that Buddha and Jesus were Highly Evolved Beings from Another Dimension?

I am saying that these are ideas not widely accepted or practiced in humanity's culture at the time.

Or even today.

Or even today. Those who spoke them were inspired.

So were they HEBs or were they not?

164

It will serve no useful purpose here to singly identify any and every individual within humanity's history who received their inspiration from an entity who birthed as a Highly Evolved Being embodying on your planet—or who, in fact, was one.

I'm asking because, given the information in this dialogue, some might think you are inferring that the great teachers and philosophers and messengers of our past—from Lao Tzu to Socrates, Buddha to Jesus . . . from Hildegard of Bingen to Julian of Norwich, two hundred years later . . . and other models and teachers both before and after these men and women—were Highly Evolved Beings from Another Dimension. Is that what you are inferring?

You see how this has already become a distraction from their message? It is almost as if the wonder and the glory of their modeling, the insight and the wisdom of their message, should somehow be considered in a different way because it may have been inspired by a Highly Evolved Being, or because they, themselves, may have been such a being, come from another dimension and born to humanity to assist the species.

Yet why should the *origin* of any message or modeling have more importance than the *content*?

The effect of HEBs having offered inspirational assistance in your evolutionary process was not intended to cause you to question your past, but to inspire you to create a glorious future.

Truth is truth, no matter what the source.

Leaving the question of our distant past, then, let me ask you this: Are such beings embodied on our planet now?

It would likewise serve no useful purpose to follow that line of inquiry.

If I said, "Yes," you would want to know immediately the identity of that entity. If I said, "No, not at this time in your history," you would then ask me to identify who was the most *recent* one in your past.

In all cases, to identify anyone among you, past or present, as a member of an awakened species from Another Dimension could in some people's minds invalidate some very important messages that humans have at least partially embraced—or, in the reverse, could inordinately elevate every word they spoke or wrote, turning them into the next thing you choose to believe in, instead of *yourself.*

Now *that* hit home.

It was meant to. There would be no point in Highly Evolved Beings seeking to help humanity if all they did was cause humanity to start seeking help from *them*.

The idea is for human beings to gain an awareness of Who They Are, not to *substitute*, for that, an awareness of who someone else is.

Yes, our religions have already done that. We don't need the process repeated.

You do not.

The purpose of the entire mission in which HEBs seek to assist humanity is not to replace humanity's magnificence with their own, but to enhance humanity's magnificence with a well chosen word or idea here or there, offered to your species for its consideration.

Therefore it has been said (and I offer a gentler version here): "If you see the Buddha walking down the street, run away from him."

I never did understand that saying.

If he looks like a Buddha, walks like a Buddha, talks like a Buddha, and acts like a Buddha, he must not be a Buddha, but a fake, simply seeking your attention and adulation. Because a true Buddha would want nothing from you, least of all recognition of *his* greatness, and desire only for your own self-realization.

Wow, I see that. And this is a second wonderful answer to my question a while back about myself, and others who may self-select to help awaken the species, being tempted to show up in grandiose form.

Even if ego tempted one to do that, a deeper awareness would make it clear that it would defeat the whole purpose of accepting the Third Invitation.

It would, indeed. And for the same reason, identifying any HEB visiting Earth in the past or in the present would defeat the whole purpose of that rare visitation.

I get it. I won't press for that information, then—although I have to say, you've certainly roused my curiosity.

Of far more benefit to you will be to satisfy your curiosity about when your entire population on Earth will decide to live as a truly awakened species. That's what HEBs would enjoin you to be curious about.

27

Is it possible for me to understand, in "layman's terms," the metaphysics of all that we have been discussing?

Yes, it is. The question is whether you have the patience for it and the interest in it.

It can be helpful to you in expanding your understanding of yourself, your multi-dimensional universe, and even God, but it could feel a bit like a post-graduate class here for a moment.

Go. I'm all ears.

Simply consider this: Life everywhere is composed of far more space than matter.

(This is easily observable with either a microscope or a telescope. Not surprisingly, the universe and a grain of sand look exactly the same, depending upon the degree of the sand's magnification. The macrocosm and the microcosm are essentially identical.)

Now when pure energy—the primal expression of Life that we will call the Essential Essence—coagulates, it transforms into what would be called, in human terms, "matter."

Because these coagulations are vibrating or vac-
illating at a sufficient speed, the particles constantly
move. They not only vibrate or rotate in place, they
also move through space, propelled by the energy
of their spin—not unlike a top moving across a table
as it spins.

These countless particles can move so fast (in
relative terms) that they appear to be neither here
nor there, but everywhere at once, thus creating
the illusion of solidity—or what you would call, that
which is "physical."

You can watch the blades of a fan or the spokes
of a bicycle wheel producing exactly this same illusion. The illusion of solidity.

I got it. So you're saying that by simply *reducing* the
vibratory frequency, or speed, of their Essential Essence,
HEBs from Another Dimension *de-solidify*, or "disembody."

That's right. All they have done is dramatically
slow the spin of their energy particles, thus expanding the time it takes for those particles to get from
one point to another in their vibratory pattern.

You suddenly see the space between the particles, even as you would see the space between the
spokes of a bicycle wheel if the power that's spinning it is turned down.

(By the way, take a look at the universe, or any
of its galaxies, from a great enough distance and all
you will see is a Big Wheel.)

Now, should the space between the spokes of a
bicycle wheel be sufficiently enormous (as it would

feel to you if you were the size of a microbe and your perspective was therefore myopic), all you would see for a very long time—until the next spoke of the wheel came by—is empty space. In effect, while you are waiting and watching for the next spoke, the solidity will appear to have disappeared. What you do not know is that *it was never there to begin with.* It was merely the speed of the spokes moving past your line of sight that created the *illusion* of solidity.

When a Highly Evolved Being de-physicalizes, the time between the HEB's energy cycles is so long (in relative terms) that the space between its vac-illations is (also in relative terms) enormous—and what once appeared to others as a solid physical form no longer has that appearance. The entity seems to have "dis-appeared," as it cannot be seen in its entirety unless viewed from a huge (to you, unfathomable) distance.

The formula is simple:

Time + Space = Appearance.

If you could stand back far enough from the entire universe—and the *universe* of universes— you would see the Body of God.

So what physicists are now conjecturing about is true? There is more than one universe?

Yes. The cosmos is a multiverse, not a universe.

So to use a well-worn turn of phrase, *we don't know the half of it.*

To be more accurate—and perhaps coin a new phrase—you don't know the one-hundredth of it. But Highly Evolved Beings from Another Dimension understand the metaphysics of existence perfectly, and therefore are clear that they neither exist nor cease to exist simply because of the frequency rate of their energetic vibration. They merely appear to be, or not to be, "physical."

"To be or not to be, that is the question."

Precisely.

HEBs know that they exist always and forever as vibratory individuations of the Essential Essence, and that all they are doing is regulating the fluctuations of their energy, altering their vacillations to become seen or not seen, visible or not visible, what you would call "physical" or "non-physical," as it suits their purpose.

How simple. They never really "embody" or "disembody," they simply *always are*. They always are *both*. And they fill more, or less, space—in a sense, expanding or contracting themselves—by merely altering the speed of their energetic vibration.

And God is so huge, because of your energetic vibration, that you can't be seen at all! That doesn't mean you're not there, it just means you're so *expanded* that the space between your energy particles makes you invisible.

Brilliant. You've got it! A metaphysical explanation of "God"!

You and *everything* are the energy particles of God. And the huge space between the giant spinning particles of the cosmos is mirrored in the huge space, in relative terms, between the particles of which *you* are comprised.

You do understand—yes?—that if you look at your own body underneath enormous magnification, what you will see is exactly what you see when you look up at the night sky? You would see that both you and the cosmos are 99% space.

Do you imagine this similarity to be a coincidence?

If you took the air out of every person on Earth and left only their energy particles, the entire human race would fit into a child's marble.

This is mind-boggling.

And very helpful to understand

Most humans think of themselves as what they see and experience when their energy particles are moving at top speed.

You think you are a body, rather than a soul *creating* a body through a simple metaphysical manipulation.

When a person's energy particles are moving at top speed, you say that person is "living." And when their energy is moving at very slow speed, you say they have "died."

Yet death does not exist. You never cease to be, you simply change form. Actually, when you "die" you become more *expansive*.

So I *never* "de-physicalize." I am *always* a conglomeration of energy particles, and I never cease to be that. That's what you mean when you say that death does not exist! Whether I am "physical" or "metaphysical" is simply a matter of how *expanded* is the time that it takes for the particles I am to spin; of how far apart, on the Space/Time Continuum, my particles are! And this is simply a function of the speed at which they rotate, and thus move around each other.

You see? You asked if you could understand, in layman's terms, all of this, and I said "yes"—and you have.

But my body continues to exist in physicality when the soul departs. It's either buried or cremated or in some other way disposed of, but it doesn't just disappear.

No, it simply ceases to exist in its present physical form. Eventually it dissipates.

But it seems to me that it's *more* "integrated" with the planet. My "dead" body eventually decomposes and becomes part of the larger composition of the Earth in which it is buried. Or, if it was cremated, changes form instantly into the dust of which the Earth and the Cosmos is made. But it doesn't disintegrate.

That is correct. The body that you have does not disintegrate, it RE-integrates. It eventually becomes so fully integrated with the physicality around it that it, ironically, seems to disappear. It actually has not *dis*-appeared at all, but taken on a *new* appearance.

It now appears to be melded into, or one with, the stuff of which everything is made.

Ashes to ashes, dust to dust.

Exactly. And the particles are then gathered by the soul that inhabited that body, and reunited with the Mind and the Spirit to become, once again, the three-part Self. This is the Resurrection of the Body, of which much has been written.

But that doesn't happen instantly, as it does with Highly Evolved Beings. That's my point. This process takes time.

If you look at it within the framework of that illusion, yes. But looked at from another vantage point, the viewpoint of the soul when in metaphysical form, it's all happening at once.

The energetic expressions that you call your body and your mind travel with the soul—indeed, are parts of the soul—through all eternity. What your mind, in its limited understanding, calls body and mind are merely aspects of the soul's energy, vibrating at frequencies that cause them to be experienced and expressed in particular ways.

You are a three-part being—body, mind, and spirit—and you never, ever are anything less or anything else. As you move from the metaphysical to the physical and back again, you simply disintegrate and reintegrate these aspects of Who You Are.

To help you understand how such a thing is possible, think of what you call "white light." This is actually a combination of lights of different wavelengths in the electromagnetic spectrum. If you send white light through a dispersive prism, you will see its spectral colors, which are its constituent parts.

Now think of physicality as the "prism" of Ultimate Reality. When the soul passes through the prism into physicality, it breaks into its constituent parts: body, mind, and spirit. When it passes back through the prism the other way—or as humans put it, when you "pass away"—the soul becomes one element again.

That one element is You.

28

I find myself wanting to insist that all of these things— all of this process that you've just explained so well to me—requires *time* and *space* for it to take place. And you keep saying that there are no such things as Time and Space. I'm trying to reconcile this.

I see that you *really* want to get into the cosmology of life deeply.

Sorry. It's as I said before. I guess I can't understand— or accept—any of this unless I understand and accept all of it.

That's okay. That's good. *Keep being skeptical.* You're doing it on behalf of many of your brothers and sisters. This is about awakening the species.

While I've explained much of this to you before, some may be coming to this for the first time. And others, like you, may have stored in the farthest reaches of their mind, and forgotten, what I've said to you before.

So let's get into it at least briefly here, and if you want more detail, you can go back into our previous dialogues and re-read them.

Okay, because what I'm getting now is that the process by which both humans and even Highly Evolved Beings in Another Dimension evolve, experiencing themselves at higher and higher levels, seems to require time. So yes, I do need a refresher on this. And I think it will help me, as a practical matter, in the living of my life.

> It can and will, yes.

So are you saying that even Highly Evolved Beings live within what you describe as the "illusion" of time?

> They do, indeed. The difference is, they *know* it is an illusion, and so they focus on the illusion inter-mittently, as described a bit earlier, allowing them to use it for the purpose at hand.

This is beginning to get past me a bit; I'm starting to go under here. I mean, this feels like I'm over my head.

> Let's use an example that can get you out of deep water.
>
> Think of a DVD of your favorite movie. The whole story is there on the disc, is it not?

Yes.

> But you don't watch it all at once. You focus the laser on the data one bit at a time. Then the next, then the next, then the next—making it seem very much as if the data actually *exists* sequentially, even

though you know better. You know it's all there at once. It's all there, all the time.

Now if humans, as infants in the cosmic community of sentient beings, can figure out how to do that, what do you think Highly Evolved Beings can do with the data of the giant disc called the universe?

You've given me this illustration before, and I'd forgotten about it. Thanks for bringing it back to my awareness. And what a great analogy. I think I'm above water again.

Good. So you are beginning to understand the illusion. But most humans do not know that time and space are illusory, and thus imagine that they are constricted by them, and must obey the "laws" of time and space.

It is like anything in life, really. When you know the "rules," you can disobey them. Or you can use them to produce whatever effect you wish.

This is what *I* do on a grand scale, of course. And this is what any being who *acts* like God does as well.

So are you seriously suggesting that we ignore the laws of time and space? Isn't that rather like suggesting to a person who entertains delusions of grandeur to go ahead and jump out of an airplane without a parachute because he can just ignore the law of gravity and can fly?

I'm not suggesting that you ignore any of the laws of the universe as you understand them. I'm suggesting that you *use* them.

How do we use them? And how would the average person even know that they *are* illusions? They sure seem real enough to us.

> They're supposed to. That's the whole point of them. They were created to produce a Contextual Field within which you could express and experience your Self at the highest level—and then the next highest level, and the next, and so on through all of your life . . . and all of your *lives*.

But my two questions still stand. How do we use these illusions, and, excuse me, but how can we even know that *are* illusions? Personally, I love the DVD analogy, but is there any way that this can be proven?

> You best use the illusions by understanding and realizing that time and space are not what they seem, and that you can react and respond to them in a variety of ways to produce a variety of experiences.
>
> For instance, have you ever noticed that "time flies while you're having fun"? Conversely, have you ever noticed that three weeks can seem like three months when you're waiting for something special or important?

Yes, and I've also noticed that nothing makes me more productive than "the last minute."

That's right. You can accomplish more in four hours than you might normally do in two days when it's the last four hours you have!

Now here is how understanding this can become practical: You can accomplish more in conserving Earth's resources, protecting its environment, improving human conditions on the planet, and experiencing your own personal transformation in the next ten days than you did in the previous hundred, and in the next ten years than you did in the previous century, if you choose to.

The first step in making this possible would be to accept that Time is an illusion, and not let yourself be limited or discouraged by "how little time" it seems you have—or allow yourself to become apathetic because of "how *much* time" you think you have.

Let the assessment of your abilities and the setting of your goals have nothing to do with time. Free yourself from those artificial constraints. You really can, as your old saying goes, begin doing right now what you have been putting off until "tomorrow."

As for proof, in terms of physics and not simply DVD analogies, that time as you understand it *is* an illusion: You are aware, are you not, that if you were to take a ride in a spacecraft and travel far enough fast enough away from Earth, and if you could turn around and look back at Earth and gaze upon your brother, you would not see what is happening in his "now," but in his past, yes?

Then I could actually see myself taking off!

That is correct. If you could travel far away fast enough, you could turn back and peer into your own past.

That would mean I would exist in two places at once!

(Ahem—have you not ever talked to your "future self"?)

Similarly, if you *began* a journey from a position in deep, deep space when it was a certain "time" on Earth, and if you were able to take a snapshot of what was happening on Earth as you were racing there, what you would see at the same instant that your brother was experiencing his "now" on Earth would be *your brother's future.*

I don't think I ever understood that. How can I know this is true?

Study the work of Albert Einstein. Ask any physicist. They will tell you that there is a direct link between motion through space and passage of time.

Is this what the so-called Space/Time Continuum is all about?

It is exactly that. Space and time are not two different things, but one unified element of the cosmos; two aspects of a Single Reality.

In that Single Reality there is no such thing as past, present, and future. There is only how you're looking at The All of It. There is only the single

Golden Moment of Now, experienced from different "places" in the Space/Time Continuum.

You have told me before that everything that's ever
happened, is happening now, and ever will happen—is
happening right now. So this is what you meant.

It is.

Our experience of time is created by our place in
space, is that what you're telling me?

Yes.

Then how can we ever change things? If everything
has already happened, we couldn't change our future even
if we wanted to!

You could change the future that you, and all
those living now, *experience*. There is not just one
"future" that exists, but every possible future that
you could create.

Think of it as a game of computer chess. Every
conceivable outcome of every conceivable move is
already on the program disc. You are determining
how the game proceeds by the moves you make,
but you could put the same disc into the computer
tomorrow and play the game from scratch making
different moves, and the program would respond in
a totally different way—producing an entirely different "future" with an entirely different outcome.

In the computer chess game, all of the possible futures already exist, and you are deciding which of those outcomes you will experience, based on the moves that you make.

Well, there's another wonderful analogy! Even my limited mind can now begin to conceive of reality in a new way.

You and those who will live after you can and will "change" the future (you are merely *selecting* the future that you choose, based on the moves that you make!), affecting all those living with and after *them*—and on and on, through the ages.

When I said that everything that ever happened, that is happening now, and that ever will happen, is happening *right now*, I meant "everything" in the biggest sense of the word. This includes every possibility and every outcome and every future you could imagine—and some of which you have not even begun to conceive.

So the future is assured! We know that it exists, in some form or another, depending on what "moves" we make.

The future *is* assured. But *which* "future" you experience is up to you.

We are not talking "predestination" here. There is no One Single Future into which you have no choice but to step. There is The Future that you are creating and experiencing, based on the choices and actions you take.

You have so often said, "There is more going on here than meets the eye," and you were not kidding. You meant that *literally*.

> I did, indeed. And now you have grown in your perception to the place where you can understand how I *could* mean it literally.
>
> So if you care about what *your* future will be like on Earth, you will begin creating that particular "future" by affecting and changing conditions "now."
>
> Life will never end, because Life has no "beginning" *and* no "end." But you will only experience in your present state of consciousness one life at a time. What your present lifeline brings you, and all those who are traveling alongside you through the Space/Time Continuum, depends on you and on them.

You are making me think all about it, and I remember now that much of this is found in the transcript of *Home with God*. I looked it up, and I see that there you told us clearly: "There is nothing mysterious about the universe once you look right at it, once you see it multi-dimensionally. This is not easy for you, because you have placed yourself with a body, inside of Space and Time, seeing, perceiving, and moving in the limited directions of which the body is capable. Yet your body is not Who You Are, but something that you have."

> Yes, and that is not all of what is being shared here that has been given to you by me before. But now, in this present conversation, you are pulling much of it

together in one place, capturing and re-energizing the main thrust of our previous exchanges.

You and others can use this summary here as a quick reference, a solid reminder, and a powerful tool for any person who has self-selected to awaken to the fact that they *are* awakened, and to humbly commit to assist in whatever way they may be able in the awakening of others.

29

Let me get back for just a bit to those other advanced, but not necessarily evolved, entities who live on other planets in the cosmos. You said that some of them have continued to be violent, even as the young species of Earth is violent, even though they have advanced hugely in their technologies. So I have to ask . . .

Why were such sentient beings allowed to get so far along in the development of their civilization in the first place before being helped? Why weren't they approached by Highly Evolved Beings from Another Dimension when they were as young as Earthlings are now, so they could have healed or transformed their immature violent behavior?

They were, Dear One, they were.

And it didn't help? I don't get this. If you're God, and if these HEBs—what shall I call them . . . these *emissaries*—are one of many forms of Divinity, expressing and experiencing Who They Really Are by helping other life forms to evolve . . . how could such an effort not have produced a shift in the consciousness of those otherwise advanced entities, such that violence would have been simply abandoned?

Every being in the universe—and, by extension, every civilization—has free choice, remember?

The fundamental characteristic of all sentient life forms is freedom. Freedom to create any reality they choose.

Many of the civilizations that are now older did not choose, when they were as young as Earth's civilization is, to awaken to their True Identity.

But I thought that God could not fail. I mean, *at anything.* The idea that failure exists is one of The Ten Illusions of Humans. So how is it that the attempt of HEBs from Another Dimension did not inspire advanced, but not fully evolved, beings living on other planets in the Realm of the Physical to awaken to their Divinity as a matter of their own free will?

None of their efforts were without benefit. They did inspire many individual entities. But the civilization as a whole continued to choose another path. Yet—to answer your question about God "failing"—know that all sentient beings in the universe ultimately freely choose to embrace their Divinity.

They do?

Yes. The question is not whether they will freely make this choice, but whether they will do so before or after—or because—they've caused so much damage to their civilization, and the planet on which they thrived, that life as they had known it was altered forever.

In many ways, the whole *idea* is to bring an end to "life as they have known it"—but exchanging it, of course, for a new and more joyous way of life, birthed by a new and transformed way of *being*.

So it's not a question of *whether* Highly Evolved Beings existing in Another Dimension awaken those other physical species, but *when.*

You could frame it that way, yes.

What does *that* mean?

That means within the framework of your present understanding of time, you could put it that way.

Ah, yes, we just looked at this. So at some level it's already happened!

And as we've noted, nothing occurs in sequence. Everything is happening simultaneously. Your individual experience of this reality appears to you to be sequential, yet the reality exists in its totality simultaneously. Life is, therefore, what you might call "sequentaneous."

Well, if the "future" has already happened, then you, as God, must know already about *everything* that's "happened." So just tell us now what the outcome is, and we can be done with all our worrying and wondering and fretting and trying . . .

I won't be doing that.

Why, because it's all a *big secret* and you're not supposed to let the cat out of the bag?

> No, because every *conceivable* outcome has already occurred, and the one that *you*, and those of you in this life, will experience is the one that you will choose—and I will not do anything to preempt that choice, or the making of it by you. I will always leave you a choice in the matter.
>
> This is true Godliness. This is the truest experience of Divinity. And this is the experience I desire for you.

Okay. I'm going to accept that, and let it go. So for now, can we talk within the context of a sequential reality; the reality I am experiencing in my life?

> We can, and we are.

Good. Within that framework, I am now understanding that Highly Evolved Beings have chosen to help Earthlings to awaken to Who We Really Are. I understand as well that we have a choice to awaken before we damage our civilization and our planet such that "life as we know it" is disassembled and disappears.

I assume that if we do not awaken now, during this early stage of our cosmic development, we could wind up living in this lifeline essentially as many older species in the physical realm do, becoming more and more violent even as we become more and more advanced.

Those last thirteen words are a description of how things are going on your planet now.

Yes. We *are* becoming more and more violent even as we become more and more advanced. That is the sadness of it.

As we develop our technologies and our weapons of mass destruction even further, we could become so violent that we could completely self-annihilate.

No. Not completely. The Superconscious Will of your species will not allow it. No species ever totally, utterly, and completely self-annihilates. You may even have to find a way to migrate to another inhabitable location in the cosmos, with but a handful of humans, but the species will never totally self-annihilate.

You have come very close, though. Human civilization has already gotten very close.

Are we talking Lemuria here? And Atlantis?

We are.

So we have our work cut out for us here. We may not completely disappear as a species, but we can do plenty of damage if that's what we choose.

That is correct. Currently that's not what most of humanity is choosing. Yet many sentient beings do things that bear no relationship to what they choose. Remember our children-with-matches analogy?

Yes.

Very young children who light matches and start a fire that burns the house down did not choose to do that. That can be the outcome of what they did, but it is not what they chose. And the only reason the house burned down is because the fire department didn't arrive on time.

In your case—in the case of your civilization—the fire department has arrived.

That's what the Third Invitation is all about. You are the fire department; you and others like you on Earth who are going to self-identify as being committed to assist in the awakening of the species.

If that's the case, I need to ask that we now turn this conversation into a look at something more personal. Remember when you said I want to be careful not to focus so much on the fascinating aspects of all we've been discussing, that I lose my focus on what's important for me to get out of this on a personal level, to assist in my own further awakening?

Yes.

And you actually mentioned, then, the topic of full integration, which is exactly what I feel called to talk with you about now. And I think that others who have self-identified may have the same question I do—or issue, if it's not unkind to them to put it that way.

Go ahead. I'm here.

30

How do I, how do they, integrate all of this?

We've been given some great insights here about how humans could live if we were an awakened species, but the question now is, how do we make this work in everyday life?

If I'm in the fire department, I need to change my *own* behaviors before I can begin to think of producing some kind of change on the planet. Gandhi had it right. I need to be the change I wish to see. But I have not been able to do that to my satisfaction. I'm finding that information is one thing, integration is another.

The great sadness of my life is that I haven't been able to fully integrate all that I have come to know and understand as a result of our conversations. I haven't been able to make it a consistent part of my life. I mean, my daily *interactions*, not just my daily *thoughts*.

And here's what I *don't* want to do. I don't want to share with others messages that cannot be actually lived and demonstrated. I'm not interested in pie-in-the-sky, impractical, unworkable, or non-achievable evolutionary goals.

These goals are achievable, I promise you. Regular, normal human beings have lived their lives in the ways that have been described here.

That may be so, and I am so very glad to know that, but I can tell you that in my experience this has been a huge challenge. I hear you say that I am Love, for example, and that we are *all* Love; that Love is what we're made of, that it is Who We Are. Well, you know, I *think* I'm a loving person, I *want* to be a loving person, I *try* to be a loving person, but far too often I say something or do something or *am* something that is just plain and simply not very loving.

Either I'm not loving the Earth, or I'm not loving myself, or, saddest of all for me, I'm acting in a way that is not very loving toward another.

I want to get above that. I want to move past it. I want to go beyond it. I'm entering the first third of my seventh decade on this Earth and I'm really wanting to see more progress. How *long*, oh God, how long will this take?

You're being very hard on yourself. Many who know you would say you're a very loving person. And so is everyone who has been drawn to this conversation, or has found themselves following this dialogue "by chance."

It is true, indeed, of everyone on the Earth. You are, all of you, my wonderful children, growing and becoming more and more of your True Divine Self every day.

It is as I told you in our very first conversation . . .

You are goodness and mercy and compassion and understanding. You are peace and joy and light. You are forgiveness and patience, strength and courage, a helper in time of need, a comforter in time of sorrow, a healer in time of injury, a teacher in times of confusion. You are the deepest wisdom and the highest truth; the greatest peace and the grandest love. You are these things. And in moments of your life you have known yourself as these things. Choose now to know yourself as these things always.

I am trying. I am really trying. We all are. But I don't seem to have found the formula. I don't seem to have found a way to consistently be who I want to be, who I know I am, when daily life presents itself. Can you help me? I feel like I'm floundering here.

You might begin by letting this very conversation be of lasting benefit. Read the transcript that you have made of it often. Pay attention to the list of sixteen ways in which an awakened species behaves. Place particular focus in your personal life on Item numbers 1, 2, 3, 4, 8, 12, 14, 15, and 16.

Thank you. I will do that. I will do exactly that. But is there anything else you can tell me, any other ideas you might offer?

Yes. Number one, see your whole life as the process, not just a small period within that whole. So do not seek to complete the integration of all that you have come to understand within the next year or month or week or day. Let your process take the time it will take.

That's not what I would call excitedly motivating to a person who is impatient.

Impatience can be not so beneficial if you let it stop you from acknowledging how far you have come and how fast you have done so, and letting *that* inspire you about your tomorrows.

In other words, be kind to myself.

In other words, be kind to yourself. Notice where you've been earlier in your life, where you were just a few years ago, and where you are now. Your progress has been exponential. You've not been moving forward at a 1-2-3-4 rate, you've been moving forward at a 2-4-8-16-32 rate.

This is true of all those who are following the conversation here. It is, in fact, why and how they have come to do so. They are not following this exchange "by chance." They have brought themselves to this experience. All of you are now stepping into The Perfect Time for Advancement.

It's going to be easier as you move forward. The biggest part of the mountain, the toughest climb, is behind you.

Thank you. Thank you for telling us that. But could you give me any practical tools, any *methods* or approaches I could use to more fully integrate all that I know to be true? I'm searching for *congruence* here. I don't want to just talk a good game; I want to walk the talk.

And you don't think that you do.

Every so often, maybe. Every once in a while, when I'm in a really good space. But I want to do it every day. I yearn to do it all the time.

You *are* doing it all the time, don't you see? Your struggle is part of the process. It's *part* of doing it all the time. If you weren't walking the talk all the time, you wouldn't pay ten seconds worth of attention to any of this.

The whole world is going through an evolutionary shift right now, and you're not immune to that. You're part of it. You're actually part of that which is creating it. All of you who are engaged here right now have self-selected to be part of that.

So have patience with yourself and have patience with the process. You're all going exactly where you all seek to go, and you're all getting there, and you are—each of you—sweetly and gently taking others there with you, as they see the changes in you and feel inspired to create changes in themselves.

If they saw you showing up *all at once* as The Perfect Example of An Awakened One, they might admire *you*, but they would never see *themselves* there. Don't you see, then, that you are going through your struggles on their behalf? Do you see that it serves them for you to be doing so?

Do not ask, then, for your struggles to end. Ask them to be even more evidenced, and then more visibly and successfully overcome, and in this way all of you will awaken a species that is wondering if such a process is possible—and see in you that it is.

You have a way of making everyone feel better.

Well, if I can't, who can?

Cute. You really can be cute, you know that?

So I've been told.

But really, couldn't you give us some tools here? Some methods we could use to at least keep this process of our personal evolution moving forward?

You do know that there is no "right way" to the mountaintop.

Yes, I know that. You've made that clear many times. But surely you can offer us some options, some things we might consider.

With that caveat, here are five, then . . .
Share Your Process.
As spoken of in an earlier part of our exchange here, and referred to again just a moment ago, share openly and authentically with those whose lives you touch both your struggles and your progress on the path to full awakening. The choice to do so is both empowering and emancipating, unshackling in an amazing way the Will Within to express the Divinity that is yours, and liberating in others their own desire and ability to also do so.
Create a Reason.

The challenges of the path you have chosen may, on more than one day, hardly seem worth confronting unless you accord them greater meaning than the simple triumph over them. The question must be asked, "Why?" Then your answer must be given.

I tell you this: Your path is not without purpose in the heavens. For every soul which would grow to know in its experience what it has always understood in its awareness serves not only its own agenda, but the Superconscious Will of the Collective, advancing the evolution of a species even as its individual progress is attained, for it shall leave in the wake of its advancement the ladders and stepping stones by which those who follow may do so ever more rapidly.

Express Gratitude.

This is the most powerful tool you could be given. Gratitude can be a selected energy, and not merely an autonomic response. When one actively chooses to be grateful for everything presenting itself in one's life (and I do mean *everything*), it sets up an energetic signature that washes over and impacts the energy of whatever is now arising. This can transmogrify (defined as: "To transform, especially in a surprising or magical manner") the presentation itself—to say nothing of one's entire life.

Choose a State of Being.

Do this in advance of anything you know you are going to think, say, or do. Life has very little to do with what you are doing and very much to do with what you are being while you are doing it. The surprising thing about this is that through pure intention, "beingness" is transformed from a reaction to a creation. It is no longer something that arises out of an experience, but something that you put into an experience.

And one final tool for integration . . .

Go with the soul.

Most often, you respond to whatever is happening in your life—whether it is an illness, a disappointment, a happy surprise, whatever it might be—from the logic center in your mind. You analyze the data that your mind holds regarding the experience at hand, and that is the place from which your reaction emerges.

It is possible for you to cultivate the ability to respond from the wisdom center in your soul. Here, the data regarding the experience at hand is unlimited and expansive, and includes considerations and understandings that may not have been even conceived of in the mind.

The soul is the place within which everything you know is *already* integrated, and simply awaits the outward expression of that. So take a moment whenever anything is confronting you—something that you call "good news" or something you call "bad news"—and instruct your mind to let you act as if you are out of your mind. Then notice your response emerge *without thinking*, producing a spontaneous demonstration of your soul's wisdom and awareness.

31

I love this, I *love* this. Now we're talking! Now I've got some equipment with which to finish climbing that mountain! This is *great*. And you know what? I actually came up with my own version of that last tool myself.

Really? All by yourself?

Well, it seemed like it was all by myself.

Yes, well, it's supposed to.
Go ahead.

Hmmm . . . are you saying—

—no, no, go ahead. Tell me what you came up with "all by yourself."

I guess I understood intuitively that there was one way that I could bring to my everyday life the experience of what I already know to be true. So I came up with, a few years ago, what I've come to call The Magic Inquiry. I use it to make an instant assessment of whether what I just did, am now doing, or am about to do, is . . . well, here's that word again . . . *congruent* with my deepest desire.

Before I sit down to watch a movie or walk into a social situation or prepare a meal or have a conversation with a beloved other, or do anything at all that I have judged to be of here-and-now importance, I quietly ask myself: *And what does this have to do with the Agenda of my soul?*

> That's a great question. That can open anyone to a powerful inner exploration.

Well, for me the answer has almost always become clear immediately, because I know that the agenda of the soul is to express and experience Divinity in me, through me, and as me. This instantly sets a context within which I can then create and experience the event at hand—or choose to eliminate it altogether from my doingness activity.

The reason I've taken to calling this The Magic Inquiry is that it almost *is* like magic, snapping my attention to exactly what's going on in the present moment like no other device I've found.

> Or been given.

Or been given.

I'm going to let that sit there. I'm just going to let that sit there.

> A good idea. Another good idea that's just come to you.

You're being cute again. You're doing it *again!* I like that! I like that about you. So let me just ask you what good idea I might just be given about this . . .

How can I decide ahead of time what I'm going to be before I *think* something? I mean, your fourth suggestion here . . . to choose a State of Being ahead of time, including how you are going to "be" when you're thinking of something . . . isn't that asking a bit much? I can decide what I'm going to be before I'm going to *say* something . . . I get that. And I can decide what I'm going to be before I *do* something . . . I get that, too. But I don't know what I'm going to think until I *think* it.

Am I making any sense here?

You are if you imagine that your thoughts are, most of the time, original. But the fact is, the vast majority of your thoughts are thoughts you have had before. This is because most of the events in your life are events that have happened before, in terms of type.

More often than not, when an event of a certain type occurs, you immediately think what you thought previously about such an event. Very few of your thoughts are original, because very few of your experiences are original. Your life is on Repeat most of the time.

Since you know this is true, you can decide *ahead of time* what you are going to think the next time an event of any real consequence and any degree of predictability takes place.

The Master is the one who knows and chooses the way she is going to be in her thinking—is he

going to be calm, is she going to be understanding,
is he going to be loving and accepting, is she going
to be accommodating and peaceful?—the next
time such an event occurs in his life.

I got it. And I think that at some level I always understood that. This may be why I came up with a second tool
on my own. That's a good one. Am I ever "on my own"?

No.

Well, here's a second tool that came through me, then.
I call this tool the Four Fundamental Questions of Life:
1. Who am I?
2. Where am I?
3. Why am I where I am?
4. What do I intend to do about that?
I find that when I ask these questions of myself, and
answer them anew in each moment they are asked, I move
almost immediately to a place of being . . . I hate to use this
word, because it's so overused and now almost trite, but
I'm going to say it anyway . . . a place of being "centered." I
feel centered within my Self and not nearly so intermingled
with the mini-dramas and micro-dilemmas of life.

You are "in this world, but not of it."

Exactly.

Those are two very good tools. They can really
help you look at how you are using your time—and
what you are being while using it.

And now I have even more tools! All of us here can be on our way if we use even one or two of these ideas.

> You can, indeed. And, of course, you're already on your way, but I understand your use of the phrase.
> I want to remind you that all of you are already awake. You merely need to begin acting like it. These tools can help.

This whole dialogue can help. The things we've been reminded of in the conversation with you can be immensely helpful. There can be enormous power in knowing and embracing some of the ideas found in this wonderful dialogue. Ideas like . . . "You are not your body." . . . "Survival is not your basic instinct, the expression of Divinity is." . . . "See the other as yourself." . . . "Life is eternal, and because you cannot lose your life, ever, you have nothing to lose by being compassionate, caring, and comforting in every circumstance." . . . and on and on and on.

I'm going to assume . . . I'm going to conclude . . . that if I simply used the tools I have been given in this life, if I found it possible to act more and more of the time as if I was already awake . . . I could feel free even while I'm in this body. You told me earlier that you would explore that with me. Am I reaching the right conclusion here?

> You are. Freedom is not getting what you want, it is wanting what you get.

I've heard that before.

You've heard almost everything here before. You will feel joyous and free when you simply apply in your life what you already know. And . . . to offer one *more* repetition . . . the fastest way to apply it in your life is to assist someone else in applying it in theirs.

I see the circle. I see the whole circumferential process. And I feel heard and helped here. Thank you. I feel heard and helped . . . and I think that's all that any of us needs to feel to be willing to move on.

So, having said that . . . there's one last thing. And this is something that I absolutely have to ask you about, because . . . sorry, I have to say this . . . it's something that's really bothering me after the exchanges we had here.

What's that?

What about heaven? What about coming home to *you?*
This dialogue seems to have reduced "dying" to nothing more than a process of moving from one state of being (physical) to another state of being (metaphysical). That may be useful and even fascinating at one level—but what happened to *coming home to God?*

32

Ever since the transcript of *Home with God* was published, I've been longing for your embrace, for you to hug me back into your heart. I was so looking forward to coming Home, to being with You, and with all those I've loved, when I did what I call "die." Are you telling me now that "death" is simply life going on—*endlessly*—with me switching back and forth from one form of existence to another throughout eternity?

I can understand how that could seem unappealing—but what's been said here about entities embodying and disembodying does not include the "middle chapter" of the story.

Um . . . didn't you think it should?

Yes, and I wasn't going to let you walk away from here without going over that. But I know how impatient you are, and we were moving deep into metaphysical explorations of the difference between Highly Evolved Beings and human beings, particularly as it relates to physicalizing and de-physicalizing at will, and you wanted to cover that thoroughly, so we did!

Now that this has all been explained, we can double back to what happens at the moment that you call "death."

If you hadn't asked the question, I would have brought it up.

You wait for me to ask a question before you tell me what you think it would be of enormous benefit for me to hear? *That's* interesting. What if I didn't ask the right questions?!!

Well, actually, I inspire your questions. I've been doing it from the beginning. And you listen closely to your inspirations, and act on them. So the chances of you not asking the question were pretty slim.

Well, I'm glad you inspired it, because some of those who are moving through this dialogue with us here may not have read *Home with God*. And even those who *have* may be wondering—as I was, myself, just now—where our wonderful, warm "meet up" with you, our experience of coming home again, fits into all of this.

And I realize, of course, that your wonderful description of what happens after we "die" filled an entire book, so it can't possibly all be repeated here. So I'm thinking of placing an addendum in this present text and listing of all the books that have comprised our dialogue series, with a description of the topics covered in each of them.

That's a very good idea. I wonder where it came
from . . .

I'm getting it, I'm getting it! I'm seeing how this whole
dialogue is happening here! So please give us a summary
now of how our experience of being home again with you
fits into the new revelations you've offered us here.

You've said here that human beings, too, shift from
physical to metaphysical manifestations *at will*, exactly as
Highly Evolved Beings from Another Dimension do—
only we call it "birth" and "death." Yet we think of each of
these "transitions" as what we label a *lifetime*, and we don't
experience that we leave our physical form "at will." We
experience that it happens *against* our will.

I know. That's why this was a focal point of the
conversation that you transcribed in *Home with
God*. To repeat what was said there, and in this very
conversation earlier: No one dies at a time or in a
way that is not of their choosing.

Again, I know this is not an easy concept to
embrace, but dying at a time or in a way that is not
of your choosing would be impossible, given Who
and What you are.

All of the revelations in the body of work that I have
called *Conversations with God* rest on the single premise
that we are, all of us, Individuations of Divinity. In other
words, God, manifested as humans.

And not only as "humans," as you now know. All sentient beings in the cosmos are manifestations of the Only Thing There Is.

In other words, God.

In other words, me. Yes.

And yet some of those beings, according to you, are nevertheless violent.

Yes, because all sentient beings are given Free Will, and not all use it in a way that is peaceful.

On the other hand, not all sentient beings on other planets in the Realm of the Physical are violent. There are civilizations that are not.

If your own greatest proclivity is to find and create peace, gentleness, and love in your life, and to place it in the lives of those around you, these other sentient beings resonate with you from afar.

They can feel my energy from that distance?

Absolutely. The energy that emanates from the core of your being reaches deep into the cosmos, extending to infinity. Your own scientists are now developing instruments that can receive interstellar signals from deep space. Members of advanced civilizations in the physical dimension have become such "receiving stations" themselves. And when they identify a particular source of that energy which you call peace, it resonates with how they experience themselves. These civilizations then will reflect that back to you, magnified, to signal to you that you are not alone, and are being supported in your experience.

Some people I am very close to feel very certain that such civilizations exist, and call them "star family."

That is an apt description. And members of this family are very happy to know that Highly Evolved Beings from Another Dimension are also offering you assistance, often in a more direct way that eliminates the gap between your planet and others in the physical realm, given that HEBs have overcome the artificial limitations of time and space.

Now—to get back to the subject at hand—when those of you in the Realm of the Physical disembody, you simply re-identify. I have said to you before that death is merely a process of re-identification.

In other words, during our life on Earth we have actually been living a "case of mistaken identity."

Exactly. And after what you call "death" you come alive to Who You Really Are, and you do return to what you've called "home"—rejoining, first, with all of your loved ones, then reuniting with The All.

And I mean that you *literally* reunite. You meld into me, and you have the experience—not just the knowledge or the awareness, but the *experience*—of our Singleness and Onlyness.

I did describe exactly how this happens in the dialogue that we had which you turned into the book, *Home with God*.

Yes, and this reminder is very helpful here.

Good. You will remember, then, that it is after the Moment of Mergence with me, after the full experience of our Oneness, that you "unmerge" with me, or *emerge*, if you please. You are then, in a very real sense, "born again" as your individual soul.

Why I would leave you? Why would I separate from this perfect union with God if this is what I have been longing for all the time? Please explain this to me again.

What your soul longs for is the *expression* of your Divinity. Once you know it fully again, once you have re-membered—that is, experienced your Self once again as a member of the Body of God—you will be overcome by a natural yearning to *express* that.

This is God's fundamental desire: To *evince* Myself. To not merely be aware of Myself, but to express Myself.

I do this by individuating Myself, so that I may evince and express every single part of me.

The part of Me that You Are will then be given the choice to either return to the physical life you've just left (you would be described as having had a "near death experience"), or move on to the Realm of the Spiritual, then to return to the Realm of the Physical in another moment.

All of this happens in the blink of an eye, of course, if you're observing it from within the illusion of sequentiality. In Ultimate Reality it is all happening simultaneously.

And those other life forms we have been discussing choose to go to that "Other Dimension"?

Yes. This is the third realm in the Kingdom of Heaven—the Realm of Pure Being, as you have conceptualized it.

Do we humans not have the option to exist in the Realm of Pure Being when we emerge from Oneness with you?

Yes, you do. You can go on experiencing your eternal Life in the Realm of the Spiritual, in the Realm of the Physical, or in the Realm of Pure Being.

Then why wouldn't I choose to exist in that Other Dimension? Why wouldn't I choose the Realm of Pure Being? After all of the wonderful ways you've described it, why in the world would I choose to come back *here*?

Because you desire to experience completion of that portion of The Journey of the Soul, which can only be undertaken in *your* dimension, the Realm of the Physical.

For this reason you will consider it a blessing to be here, right where you are now.

And, of course, it *is* a blessing. And it becomes even more of a blessing when you choose to bless others by your being here.

It is during this next period on Earth that some of you will self-select to do exactly that, intentionally. This is all part of the awakening of the species. This is all part of the Third Invitation.

33

Your quick summary here of your very detailed previous conversation with me about the after-life experience makes it more and more apparent to me that a key element—I mean, a *vitally* important element—of the process of awakening is understanding that life has no end . . . ever, ever, *ever.* Because when we understand this, and live it, everything changes.

The complete *Home with God* transcript is a remarkable text that could alter one's whole understanding of life, and that could bring wonderful comfort to any person or family member of a person facing end-of-life circumstances, so I hope that everyone will read it.

And while this statement about life never ending has now been made over and over again, I'm not sure that the real importance of it has been emphasized. This is more than a random and interesting metaphysical fact. This is a critical foundational understanding.

Yes. All that you see around you is nothing more than energy, expressing in different ways. Energy can neither be created nor destroyed. It always was, is now, and always will be.

What you call "life" and "death" is the Essential Essence manifesting as You, simply changing form.

Now the movement of life—what you call its activity and progress—is simply a process of energy exchange. The difference between the dimension in which you live, which is the physical realm, and the Other Dimension is that in your dimension the exchange of energy is sometimes a violent process, whereas in the Other Dimension it never is. *Never.*

And that brings up, again, what you've referred to here over and over again as "another dimension," and the "highly evolved beings" who are supposedly helping us now.

Not supposedly. Actually.

Okay, actually. So how is that happening? Assuming that such beings actually exist—

—that is not an assumption, that is a fact.

Given that such HEBs exist, where are they from? What is this "other dimension" you keep talking about?

There is an entirely different community of beings living in an entirely different way in what you would consider an entirely different universe.

Let me get clear here. Are you talking about an alternate reality—or what has been called a "parallel universe"?

Some in your world have used those words to describe it, yes.

Is this parallel universe is a "mirror image" of our own, simply reversed?

No. "Parallel" does not mean "identical." It means "along side of."

What you are now terming here a Parallel Universe exists side-by-side with the universe with which you are familiar, but it is in no way identical, or even nearly the same. That is why it has been referred to here as Another Dimension.

A metaphysical dimension.

A dimension in which, as we explored earlier, entities express themselves as metaphysical or physical, depending on—

—I know, I know . . . *what serves their purpose*, which, you told us earlier, is "to assist all sentient beings in the Realm of the Physical in the understanding, expressing, and full experiencing of themselves as who they really are."

Tell me this. Why would HEBs choose to come *to Earth*, where the species is so young and apparently so unable to learn or unwilling to embrace, even after *millennia*, the simple, basic formula we have been offered here for producing a wonderful life?

Why not go somewhere else to help a species to awaken? Why not go to a planet where the entities are far more advanced, and may be just a few steps away from embracing the understandings that it takes to fully awaken?

> Some do. Your planet is not the only place that Highly Evolved Beings from Another Dimension have visited.

Well, good. At least then they don't have to confront failure after failure among one of the youngest species in the cosmos.

> There is no such thing as "failure" in the experience of Highly Evolved Beings. The simple commitment to undertake anything, and the actions and activities involved in doing so, provide all the sense of achievement or accomplishment that a HEB desires.
>
> It is the best and highest expression of Self for which a being at this level of consciousness yearns. It is not necessary for the outcome of that expression to take a particular form for the experience of the expression to be validated, justified, or celebrated.

What a point of view. What a healthy, *healthy* point of view.

> Have you never done anything for the sheer enjoyment of it? Does a specific result have to emerge from everything you undertake in order for it to have been "fun" for you?

No, no, of course not. But something as important as helping to awaken an entire species would probably not fall into my category of a simple but pleasurable passing of the time. I mean, I would probably attach some significance to the outcome.

And by the way, this is not an idle consideration for me over here. You have extended to us here a Third Invitation, and I am embracing and accepting it with no small sense that I would like to be at least minimally successful.

> If you're going to make it an outcome-oriented undertaking, you're going to make it very tough on yourself before you start.
>
> You'll be watching your own every move, weighing your own every word, worrying about how in the world you can achieve what you hope to experience within yourself, nervously preparing your Plan B if your initial approach does not produce the outcome you desired, and then plunging ahead with the project to transform yourself, completely oblivious of the metaphysical impact of all these less-than-joyful energies you've projected into the space.

Heavens, I never thought about things that way.

> I know. That's the point. It's being brought up here to help you change your way of thinking.
>
> I'm going to invite you to redefine what you call "success" in your full awakening.

I'm listening, I'm listening.

Success in fully awakening is knowing that you are already awake and simply don't know it, or haven't accepted it.

And so we have come full circle from what you said at the beginning of this conversation.

We have, because it is one of the most important messages with which I could both begin and end all meaningful interaction with you.

Awakening is not about changing yourself, it is about changing your thinking *about* yourself. It is about knowing that you are—as I said to you here earlier—whole, complete, and perfect exactly as you are right now.

Your personal transformation is about *adding* to what you are now, not about *subtracting* from what you are now.

Success in any area of your life is not found in producing what you think you must produce on your journey, it's found in the love, the joy, the happiness, and the sense of True Self that you experience—and that others experience in their life because of you—along the way. That alone can produce the rest of what you think you are "supposed to" produce.

You're saying it's the journey, not the destination. That's an old saw. That's nothing new.

This whole discourse is nothing but a reminder. One Big Reminder.

Everything here you've heard before, known before, even experienced before. The purpose of all of our conversations is, and has always been, the same: To transform you into a person who knows that you already know—and simply haven't accepted it.

That's why everything you've heard from me, everything you've read in any of the transcripts of any of our conversations, has so often felt to you as something you have already known.

This includes the information here about Highly Evolved Beings from another place. You've known and understood that such beings are around since you were a child. None of this is new to you.

You're right. I'm totally comfortable with this. And I know they're not here to harm us. If they wanted to harm us, they could have done so in a thousand ways over a thousand years.

That's correct.

So, you're telling me that they are not goal-oriented. "Success" for them is not about producing a particular outcome.

It is not. Not in the sense that you mean. Highly Evolved Beings are "expression oriented." They seek only to express and experience Who They Really Are, and one way they do this is by offering and providing love and guidance, help and companionship to all sentient beings as those beings move through their own evolutionary process.

You are doing the same thing on Earth.

We are?

Think about it. All you're doing on Earth is helping each other, as a means of expressing and experiencing who you are. You are helping each other solve a problem, helping each other create a better life, helping each other get well, helping each other feel better, helping each other know more, helping each other experience joy, laughter, and a good time, helping each other with *something*.

You call your Earthly activities "jobs," or "occupations," but all you are doing is helping each other.

The result in both cases—the activity of HEBs and the activity of humans—is the same: energy exchange. One form of energy changes into another.

It is about *how this occurs* that we have to wake our species up to if we want the species to enhance its quality of life.

Exactly. And *why* it occurs. When you understand *why* energy exchange occurs, you will understand how to *cause* it to occur without *ever* needing to use violence.

You will then become a transformed society, and begin to create a heavenly world.

Why does it occur? What causes energy exchange to occur?

Love. The building up of energy to the point where the feeling that you define in your language as "love" magnetizes energy particles to energy particles, producing a co-mingling and an exchange.

I said earlier that humanity was One Decision Away from making the Human Venture become one of the most successful and joyous expressions of life in the cosmos.

I said that we must decide to open-mindedly, genuinely, and unrestrictedly explore—then open-heartedly, joyously, and unreservedly accept—the reality of Who We Really Are.

I see now that we can take the first steps toward fully implementing that decision with a simple formula: *Eliminate violence* and *remember to love.*

Yes, and the key to this formula, the fastest and most powerful way to make it work, is to releasing yourself, at last, from the imprisonment of your thoughts about Separation. You are not separate from anything. Not from each other, not from any form of life, and not from God.

So it comes down to this:

Eliminate Violence and Remember to Love
by releasing all thoughts of Separation.

That is really what it's about, isn't it . . .

That is really what it is about.

34

We're coming to the end of our time together here. I can feel this conversation reaching a conclusion. But speaking about Love . . . earlier in this conversation you said that Love is who I am, and that it is who we all are. Every human being. Now you are saying that what we have to do is "remember to love." Yet if all human beings already *are* Love . . . then what is there to remember?

> How to love. You are invited to remember how to love, by remembering that love is your True Identity.

But I don't understand how, if Love is Who We Are, it is possible for some humans to act in ways that are very unloving. We touched on this when I described earlier how unloving *I* am so often, not to mention people who do really horrible things to each other—things I couldn't and wouldn't dream of doing in my worst moments.

> No one does anything that they consider to be unloving. Everything they do they do because they *are* loving.

What?

Remember this always: Every act is an act of love. This is true for everyone, without exception.

The killer? The rapist? The thief? The religious fanatic? The racial bigot? The political tyrant? The financial swindler? The emotional charlatan?

Look deeply now. Awakening means looking deeply.

It is the love of something that is behind every decision and action of every sentient being.

All you have to do to understand why some person or group has done something is to ask: What do you love *so much* that you felt you had to do this?

The problem is not that people don't love, the problem is that people don't know *how* to love.

This does not in any way justify their actions, but it does explain them.

As a species matures, it remembers how to express love purely.

What does "purely" mean?

"Purely" means with nothing intended or needed as a return for the Self.

Pure Love is an act of selflessness, foundationed in the Self's awareness that it needs, requires, must demand nothing to be perfectly happy.

This is the Natural State of Godliness—which, incidentally, is why God requires, demands, and commands nothing at all of anyone . . . least of all abject subjugation or degrading, debasing, demeaning, groveling, and fearful worship.

So you know you have loved purely when there's nothing in it for you. Or when it is not only not to your *benefit*, but actually non-beneficial to you.

> Such a thing would be impossible. Every pure expression of Love brings benefit to the lover, in that it brings all those who purely love the highest and fullest experience of Who They Really Are that it is possible for life to provide.
>
> The ultimate purpose of Life Itself is the ultimate experience of Divinity Itself through the ultimate expression of Love Itself, which is the ultimate definition of God Itself.

That's beautiful. That is really beautifully put. But is it possible for a human being to express and experience this? I guess we're swinging right back into my question about integration. Is it possible for me to ever really feel this kind of love?

> Not only is it possible, every human being has done so. There is not a human being on the planet who has not felt it already.
>
> Perhaps they felt it when holding a baby in their arms. Perhaps they felt this kind of love for a place, or for some physical object—even something as seemingly insignificant as a favorite pillow or a stuffed animal. Perhaps they have felt this kind of love for a plant or a tree, a sunrise or the night sky.
>
> Have you not ever felt love for the night sky?

I would call that awe. Awe and appreciation.

Which is the highest form of love, because it wants and needs, gets and demands, nothing in return.

Everyone has felt this kind of love. This is the love I have for you. For every single one of you.

When you love something for the sheer beauty of it, for the sheer wonder of it, for the sheer joy of it, for the happiness it brings you to feel that energy glowing inside of you and sent out from you, you are loving purely.

If you are looking to get something back as your reward for sending it out, then you are not loving something or someone else, you are loving yourself, and simply using something or someone else as a means of doing so.

Ouch. What's wrong with loving yourself? Doesn't all love begin with self-love?

Yes. But self-love is not love that is received from anything outside of the self. Self-love is love OF the Self BY the Self—for the sheer beauty, the sheer wonder, the sheer joy of the Self being who and what it truly is.

This is how God loves Godself. This is how I love ME! And this is how I invite you to love YOU.

I wish I could do that, I really do. I mean wholly. I mean completely. I mean all the time. But it's hard for me to do that with all my faults, all my foibles, all my failings.

Here we go again. I am telling you now once more, as I have told you many times before: You are perfect.

Just as you are, you are *perfect*.

Even as you see nothing but beauty and perfection in a one-day old newborn and a one-week-old infant and a one-month old baby and a one-year-old child, so do I see nothing but perfection in you.

And I would see this, by the way, if you were one *hundred* years old . . . nay, one thousand. For that would still be less than a single heartbeat in the life of the universe.

You are growing and expanding and enlarging and completing your experience of your True Self through your expression in the Realm of the Physical here on this magnificent planet you have called Earth.

We will meet in Perfect Union again when you return Home, and as I have promised you through all your lifetimes, you will never—no, not for a moment—be without me while you are away.

I love you now as I have loved you always, with a purity that asks, needs, and demands nothing in return—for You and I are Eternally One, and the experience of this is all that Our Self desires.

I am so deeply touched by that. I am touched, and renewed. Now all I want to do is apply all of this in my life.

35

I want to make this *real*. I want to make this true for me in my *experience*.

This dialogue has included some wonderful insights, brought me some perfectly-timed reminders, and given me some potentially powerful tools. And the sixteen items on the list of differences between Highly Evolved Beings from Another Dimension and humans will stand as guideposts for me on my journey, I am clear. But what I need now is to know and to feel that this idea of our awakening and our advancement as a species isn't all just a pipe dream, sounding very nice, but virtually unachievable by the average person.

I don't want to go back to "business as usual" when this dialogue ends.

Look, I have only my own experience to go on, so I tend to get a little discouraged at times like this. I get inspired by the *possibilities* and discouraged at the *probabilities*. Can you hear that?

> Of course I can. Yet if you have only your experience to go on, you should be completely *en*-couraged, not *dis*-couraged.

I don't understand. I'm just a simple human being here, not a Buddha, not a Christ, not a Lao Tzu or a Mother Mary, a Confucius or a Catherine of Genoa. Not, to place it more contemporarily, a Paramahansa Yogananda or a Mother Meera.

I know that at our basis, at our *foundation*, we are all the same—that I am "cut out of the same cloth" as all of those wonderful others—but I am not demonstrating qualities in my life that evidence this.

> Actually, you are. But we'll get to that in a minute. Right now, it is perfect that you are not experiencing yourself as doing that. Do you see this? You do see this, don't you?

I sometimes have a hard time with even that nice and apparently spiritually accurate idea. I sometimes think that telling myself that it is "perfect" that my progress is so slow in *acting* like I am awakened to the fact that I am awake is just giving myself a pass; it's a way of excusing my past and forgiving my present-moment failures.

> First of all, there is nothing to forgive—any more than you "forgive" a ten-year-old for not getting her multiplication tables right, or a four-year-old for knocking over the milk at his birthday party. You don't need to "forgive," because you understand perfectly how such a thing could happen. Understanding replaces forgiveness in the mind of the master.

I know, I know. You have made this point with me repeatedly, and I really see and appreciate the pure and wonderfully generous logic of it. But for me this "perfection" idea still sometimes feels like a fabulous "escape hatch." Somehow the idea that "it's all good" makes me not feel I need to work to make myself any better.

Well, of course, you don't "need to." Need has nothing to do with it. No one is keeping score here. No one is judging or punishing. So it's not about need. It's about desire.

Well, I can honestly say I do have desire. I truly wish to do as you have consistently invited all of us to do: Announce and declare, express and fulfill, become and experience the next grandest version of the greatest vision ever we held about Who We Are. I guess I'm just not able to see the "perfection" in taking over seventy years to even *understand* why I am here—much less step into the living of it.

Try thinking of your process in this way: If you had reached years before now the level of demonstration of, let us say, Lao Tzu, do you think you would have found yourself in the position of asking the questions that filled 3,000 pages of nine books?

Probably not.

Probably not?

Definitely not.

And so you may be among the most prolific questioners of your generation. And do you believe that the questions you have asked, and the answers you have received, have brought you benefit?

Yes. Definitely.

And have they brought benefit to others?

Perhaps. There are those who say these questions and answers have, so I guess if I am to believe them, the answer is yes. I don't want to boast about this, however. I feel humbled by it, not boastful, and I want to always feel this way.

You will feel about everything exactly the way you choose to feel, based on your decision about Who You Are, Why You Are Here, and how you wish to demonstrate that.

Can you choose to feel, then, that you're not feeling you are at the level of demonstration of Mother Mary or of Lao Tzu, or of others who have been considered masters, has been perfect?

Okay. But now I want more. I guess you could call this an increase in my desire. I want to know what it would be like for me and other members of our species to *be aware* of when we have awakened, and how we would behave if we *began acting like it.*

I have actually answered this question for you before, in previous dialogues.

232

Would you answer it again for us here, to save us from having to look it up?

Yes. If you choose to act as someone who is aware that she or he is awake, there are several things you would do.

In addition to taking the steps invited in the list of sixteen items that make us different from HEBs.

Yes, in addition to those steps.

First, you would not entertain negative thoughts in your mind. If a negative thought did happen to slip in, you would get it out of your mind immediately. You would think of something else, deliberately. You would simply *change your mind about that.*

You would also love yourself fully, just as you are. And you would love everyone else fully, just as they are. Then you would love life fully, just as it is, needing nothing to change, and seeing everything as simply something you are moving through so that you can *know* about it, and create a contextual field providing you with an opportunity to demonstrate Who You Are.

You would forgive no one and nothing ever again, out of knowing that forgiveness is neither necessary nor natural for humans who are aware that they are awake. You would clearly see that holding an idea that there is a need for forgiveness means holding an idea that an injury has occurred, and as a human who is awake you would be aware that injury is not possible in the experience of Divinity—which is

Who You Are. You would therefore replace forgiveness with understanding in your interactions with others, which would naturally lead to compassion for others as you experience a full realization of the pain, anger, or sadness they must have felt at such a high level as to cause them to abandon their true nature and behave as they did.

Also as a person who is awake, you would not mourn the death of another, not even for a moment. You might mourn your loss, but not their death—but, in fact, celebrate both the moments of love and joy that they shared with others, and the fact that they continue to live in free and wondrous expression of their evolutionary process. You would likewise neither fear nor mourn your own death, for precisely the same reason.

Finally, you would be aware that everything is energy in vibration. Everything. And so you would pay much more attention to the vibration of everything that you eat, of everything that you wear, of everything that you watch, read, or listen to, and most important, of everything that you think, say, and do, and you would immediately adjust the vibration of your own energy and the life energy that you are creating around you if you find that it is not in resonance with the highest knowing you have about Who You Are, and the experience of this that you choose to demonstrate.

That all sounds like a big order. You see? This is the moment when I get discouraged. My experience has been that these goals are very hard to reach, that these are the behaviors of masters who are very hard to emulate.

Actually, your experience has been exactly the opposite.

I . . . I don't know what you're saying here.

All of these things you have *already* experienced.

You have already had moments in which you moved away from a negative thought and simply changed your mind about something.

You have already had moments in which you loved yourself, and others, and life itself fully, and needed nothing to change—even when not everything was to your liking.

You have already had moments in which you experienced that you didn't really need to forgive someone for something they did, realizing without agreeing with or condoning what they did, why and how they could have done it.

You have already had moments in which you moved from mourning to celebrating after the death of another, and you likewise have had moments in which you truly did not fear your own death.

And finally, there have been many times when you have felt the vibration of the moment, of something you were projecting, of something you were being invited to eat or to wear or to do, and responded to that vibration by shifting the frequency of your own energy and making a new decision about whatever you were being invited to encounter or experience.

You have *all* done *all* of this. None of this is outside of your capabilities. Not a single aspect of this is beyond your ken. Nothing described here exceeds your level of mastery as a sentient being.

You merely have to decide to be this way more often.

Oh, my goodness. I never imagined it could be that simple.

It can be that simple.

Do you think I can do it? Do you think any of us can do it? I know I'm begging the question here but—

—of course you can. It is as simple as looking at a behavior that does not serve you and replacing it with a response to the invitations of life that you now choose. Have you never changed what you have called a "bad habit"?

Yes, I have. Most of us can claim some success in that.

There you are. And what made you change that habit?

I wanted to. I just decided I wanted to.

And what made you decide that?

Looking back, I guess it was just plain desire. I no longer desired to exhibit or experience the behavior. In my case, the biggest habit that I ever broke was smoking. I smoked for over twenty years, and I'd gotten up to a pack-and-a-half a day. Then one day I just decided to stop. I stopped cold. I think "cold turkey" is the phrase that's used. One day I smoked, and the next day I didn't. That was over thirty years ago. And it's not the only habit that I felt was disserving me that I've broken.

> So you have proven your ability to abruptly change a decades-long behavior.

Yes.

> Then your movement from a person who is awake and does not know it or act like it, to a person who is aware that you are awake and chooses to act like it, is one step, one decision, away—just as you, yourself, said here earlier in this conversation.
>
> And you can easily take that step, you can easily make that movement, because unlike breaking a bad habit, this is not even about adopting a brand new behavior. It is simply about doing what you have already done in your life, and *now doing it more often.*

You know, I never thought about it in that way. I never thought about the fact that every one of these behaviors are things I've already done. I thought of them as things I have to *achieve*, not things I'm being invited to *repeat.* I thought of them as skills I had to *acquire*, not behaviors I'm invited to *replicate*.

I see now something I never saw before. I see that I can get where I want to go more easily than I ever thought, *because I've already been there.* I know the *way* there. That's exciting to me. Wow, this has uplifted me, encouraged me!

I don't have to *reinvent* myself, I only have to *reinstate* myself, restore myself, reinstall myself in the moments of my life as I have been before.

> That is a grand awakening. Now you are awake
> to the fact that you are already awake.

There's not much more to be said here, is there?

> No, there is not.

This is it, then?

> This is it.

Thank you, God. Thank you, my dear, dear friend. I will always remember this experience, and be grateful for it until the end of my days.

> Which will never come.

Which will never come. Amen, and amen.

Epilogue

My dear, dear companions on this journey . . .

This is not easy, is it?

I mean, this journey through life.

For most of us, this is not easy. It involves sadness and tragedy in way too many moments. Happiness, too, yes. And moments of great joy, for sure. But the heaviness of the heart, and the ache of its breaking over and over again, can take its toll—that's undeniable. Even the optimist feels it some mornings upon arising and some evenings when the weight of events, and memories of events, is carried to bed.

For fifty years I've kept telling myself: "There's got to be a reason. There's got to be a purpose. This has all got to be part of a Larger Process in which we're all engaged here. Life *must* be more than a series of random events to which we're all subjected, with the Final Bell ringing at a time or in a way that we least expect."

The conversations with God that I've had since I slipped past my forty-ninth birthday (now twenty-four years ago) have convinced me this is true. And this latest dialogue—totally unexpected and packed with surprises—has confirmed everything for me.

But please, listen to me as I wave goodbye: I could be wrong about all of this.

Don't imagine for a second that I don't think about that. I think about it all the time.

Several interviewers have asked me basically the same question. Do I have any doubts about the experience I've had, or the information I've received?

I've given them all the same answer:

"The day I stop doubting is the day I become dangerous, and I have no intention of becoming dangerous."

So I want to tell *you* to doubt as well. (I'm sure I don't have to encourage this.) I want you to be clear that one of the most important messages of the *Conversations with God* dialogues is not to believe them.

Indeed, in the very first book of the nine texts we hear this in the voice of God:

"Believe *nothing* I say. Simply *live* it. *Experience* it. Then live whatever other paradigm you want to construct. Afterward, look to your *experience* to find your truth."

We do well to remain our own authority in all matters regarding the Self and the soul. No one can tell us what is true for us, and no one should try.

That said, I became very clear on what is true for me when I read the recommendations and the suggestions on how I might live my own life found in the CWG dialogue, and I couldn't help but think: "I wish someone had told me these things fifty years ago. I can't imagine a better way to live."

Yet I am very much aware that not everyone will agree. Not everyone will resonate with what has been written here. Some may consider it bizarre and outlandish; others will say it is far worse than that, labeling it blasphemous and heretical. I want you to know that I sincerely respect and honor their point of view—and all points of view sincerely arrived at, honestly held, and expressed without violence.

This is a powerful subject we are talking about here, and it is good to proceed with care. All of it is wrapped up in our relationship with The Divine—indeed, in the question of whether there even *is* a "God." And that is not a small matter.

Our understanding of all of this is significant because most human beings need and seek and sooner or later deeply yearn to find some kind of *meaning* in life. Without that meaning, without some *purpose* for it all, many of us soon find ourselves simply trudging along with that heaviness of heart I spoke of earlier.

We'll move through life trying to make the best of something we haven't even begun to understand, pushing through our days and nights engaged in increasingly aimless, valueless, senseless activities that clarify nothing, that produce little, and that generate not much more than more things to do while on our way to where, we don't know, but an eventual end that we call death, the anticipation of which offers naught but a heightened sense of what feels like the almost bitterly laughable fruitlessness of it all.

And so we yearn, and we search.

Giving all this deeper thought as I write these words, I arrive at a place of knowing that if we hold the notion that there is some sort of Higher Power in existence, our reaching clarity may very well be guaranteed.

Seek and ye shall find, God has said to all of us. *Knock and it shall be opened unto you.* We may very well remember, through our own communion with the Divine, that there *is* something greater going on here. Information may come our way that will make the "larger-ness" of all that is and all that occurs suddenly apparent. Indeed, the book you are reading could be a part of that very process, playing out right now.

I do not believe that your interaction with The Divine was ever intended to be a one-way encounter. I believe it was intended to provide you with comfort, and to produce for you a goal worthy of your dedication, of your commitment, of your time and your effort.

And so, I encourage you to engage in your own conversation with God every day, in whatever way feels natural and good to you based on your tradition or your innermost feeling. Call it prayer, call it meditation, call it inspiration, call it whatever you wish. And if my exchange with God here leads you to your own, my publishing it will have succeeded in its goal.

If you're in harmony with the *Conversations with God* material, you will find in this present text all that you need in order to move the CWG messages more fully into your life. Simply embrace and apply the sixteen items describing the differences between humans and Highly Evolved Beings, use regularly the seven tools explored in the portion of this dialogue dealing with integration, and repeat the everyday behaviors that you have already shown yourself to be perfectly capable of demonstrating. Then don't be surprised if your life changes right before your eyes.

Now let me share with you some final thoughts, written and added to this book several weeks after the writing of the main text was complete.

On November 1, 2016, I underwent surprise open-heart surgery: a quintuple bypass. I did not know I needed it until an angiogram a few days earlier confirmed my suspicion that something was going on with my old ticker. I just wasn't feeling right, and thought I'd better get myself checked out. That decision saved my life. It turns out that five arteries to my heart were blocked—one of them at 98 percent.

I am sharing this very personal information with you for a reason. Not to get your sympathy, but to get your attention.

This life we are living, this life through which you are I are walking hand-in-hand, will not go on forever. Not in its present form. Our existence is eternal, but our lives in any particular form are not.

This has been brought home to me in a powerful, powerful way. There's nothing like getting your chest sawed open, heart stopped, body put on a machine to do its blood circulating and breathing for three hours, and chest then wired shut and zipped up again, to make this message clear to you: You are not your body. Your body is something you have, not something you are. Who you are is eternal. What you have is not.

The American poet Em Claire (who I am joyously happy to say happens to be my beloved wife) captured this reality perfectly in her poem, *Precious Occurrence* . . .

I am a precious occurrence,
and I don't have long.

We are a precious occurrence.

And as long as we think we have,
we don't have long.

Too much time is being spent
running
from face to face
asking, "What is my name?"

If you don't yet know it,
or if you've forgotten,
then become still, go within
and answer it.

You are a Precious Occurrence:

Tell *us* your name.

"Precious Occurrence" *em claire*
©2008 All Rights Reserved
emclaire.love

The experience of my open-heart surgery made me think long and hard. And not for a moment or two, but from the day after the operation to this writing. What do I want to do with whatever time my present body has left?

For that matter, what do we all want to do? That is, why did we come here? What, at the end of our current physicalization, will really matter?

Have we come here to get the guy, get the girl, get the car, get the job, get the spouse, get the kids, get the house, get the better job, get the better car, get the better house, get the grandkids, get the name on the business or on the office door, get the retirement watch, get the cruise tickets, get the illness, and get the hell out? Is this really our life's formula?

Is there nothing more to be done? Was there *ever* anything more to be done?

Then I pondered this business of *awakening*. Is there actually any such thing? Are we making the whole idea up just to give us something to do other than the mundane; other than simply surviving?

Then I said to myself: *Wait a minute. You were just given a book by God. What is its most important message? Maybe you might pay attention to that.*

So I re-read this book, from first page to last. And I decided that this was its single most important message: "You are already awake. You simply do not know it."

I see this as my opportunity now. My moment not to seek to be awakened, but to commit to behaving in a way that reflects that I already am—with every thought, with every word, with every gesture, action, choice, or decision, from this moment forward.

I have self-selected. And I find myself wishing to invite you to do the same.

Now *is* the perfect time for our advancement, as individuals and as a species. And this doesn't have to be a drudgery or a burden. It can be a joy. Expressing the highest and grandest part of us every day will feel wonderful. All we have to do is get our fear and negativity out of the way.

Let's try it. Just for a week. No, just for a day. Let's watch what we think. Watch what we say. Count the times that our thought and words (about anything) are negative. Count the times that they add positive energy and good vibes to the moment, or deplete the moment of these.

Then let's accept the invitation of Divinity and say this to ourselves in front of every encounter, every interaction, every anticipated experience with another: *I have come that you may have life, and that you may have it more abundantly.*

Let's allow this to form the context of all of our intellectual, emotional, and physical expressions from morning 'til night.

If you'd like to join me on this next and perhaps most important and exciting leg on our evolutionary journey, you will find resources to assist you at www.ihaveselfselected.com.

I created these to help myself, comprised in the main of gathered messages and material from the *Conversations with God* dialogues—which have changed my life, and which promise more, and the biggest, changes yet to come.

Do you think we can make these changes? Do you think the world we touch would be better for it if we did?

Ah, but here's the real question: Why bother? This is not easy work. Setting aside centuries—no, *millennia*—of human proclivities, penchants, predilections, and propensities is not something one does overnight. It requires thinking in a new way, understanding life in a new way, speaking to others in a new way, showing up in the world in a new way.

Why go to all the trouble? Why not just get the guy, get the girl, get the car, get the job, get the spouse, get the house, get the kids, etc., and get on with a life that has no larger purpose beyond that?

Because we came here to do more than this.

We did not come here to play The One with the Most Toys Wins. We did not come here to squeak by, slinking from birth to death hoping for not much more than to sustain the least amount of damage and create the highest level of whatever we define as "happiness" and "success." Do we really think this was meant to be the Sum Total of the Earthly Experience?

That's another reason to bother, as well.

Because our world—the one you wish to leave to your children and your grandchildren—cannot continue to exist as it has, will simply not be sustainable, if "get the guy, get the girl, get the car, get the job" is all that human beings continue to do.

It is time for our species to awaken, to advance, to become aware of Who We Are and Why We Are Here and the Purpose of All Life.

Is the purpose of existence to just *exist?*

Surely not. Surely there must be more than this.

And there is. The books in the *Conversations with God* series make this very clear. That is why I use them as a resource every day of my life. I hope you will do so as well. Read them. All of them. Not because I think you'll find The Answer to Life's Biggest Mystery there, but because I believe you can find the way to Your Own Answer there. You will either agree or disagree with what is offered in these texts, but either way, you'll have moved closer to your own innermost truth.

Then you can more fully live it.

And then you will awaken the species. For the one who lives the highest and grandest innermost truth about oneself and the purpose of life cannot help but touch others in a way that gives them back to themselves, arousing them from their slumber of forgetfulness by mirroring for them their own highest hopes and grandest thoughts.

This is our invitation. This is our opportunity. This is the next step in our own evolution. And taking this next step is the purpose of all of life. For the soul expresses life through advancement, advancement, *advancement*. Expansion, expansion, *expansion*. Becoming, becoming, *becoming*. Eternally and everlastingly, and even forevermore.

This is the delight of God, embodied in every living thing. I invite you to let this be your delight as well.

With my love,

Neale Donald Walsch
Ashland, Oregon
November 22, 2016

P.S. If you find yourself energized by the Third Invitation as brought to us in this dialogue, I encourage you to notice that there are many organizations and movements around the world inviting your support in helping to awaken our species.

One such organization has arisen directly out of the messages of *Conversations with God.* It is Humanity's Team (HumanitysTeam.org), and its purpose is to send the message of oneness around the world, bringing an end to separation at last. Another is the Conversations with God Foundation (CWG.org), which works to send the messages of the CWG dialogues into the world.

And if you wish to review and study further the contents of those nine dialogues—and perhaps even participate in an Advanced Integration Program of exploration and application of its messages—you may do so at www. CWGConnect.com, which I trust will continue to be a resource long after I have celebrated my Continuation Day.

Finally, I cannot end this closing note without sharing my deepest gratitude for my wife Em, who has been my strength in times of doubt, my clarity in times of confusion, and my soul's I-Understand-You-Completely-and-Love-You-Without-Condition companion whenever she saw in me even the slightest trace of a momentary temptation to imagine that I was all alone on this Journey.

I have finally felt "Othered" in this life. I knew it was possible. I just *knew* it. But yes, I experience it as being extremely rare. My greatest happiness is that I can now tell you with absolute assurance that God's way of loving is expressible by human beings here on Earth. My dearest Em is walking evidence of that.

Em's poetic expressions have inspired me over and over again, and so I wish to close with one more of them here, that you, too, may be uplifted.

As I move back into the contemplation of the God of my understanding to which this new dialogue invites me, I find myself wanting to pose before the world the intriguing, spiritually important inquiry that Em's poem, from her published work, *Home Remembers Me*, places before us here.

I can think of no better way to conclude this latest conversation with God.

I don't know if my god is
the same as your god:

Is it made of Love?

Does it want for you what *you* want for you?

Does it come to you with arms opened,
asking nothing, but ready for anything?

Does it whisper to you of Light and of
Stillness, and point you toward *any*
of the paths that will take you there?

Does it remind you of your Seeing?
Does it remind you of your Knowing?
Does it remind you of the gentlest Lover
ever you've dreamed, soothing you
all the way down the length of your body,
to caress a weariness from your heart?

Is it ever late?

Is it ever gone?

Is it made of Love?

Addendum

About the Conversations with God series of books

There are nine books in the *Conversations with God* dialogue series, each one moving the exposition forward to increasing levels of complexity and enlarging areas of exploration.

As well, a number of supplementary volumes have been produced that offer expanded articulations of the spiritual and practical applications in daily life of the remarkable thought constructions emerging from the original dialogue.

The supplementary texts extend the original messages into vast areas of human activity, including the specific interests of younger people (*Conversations with God for Teens*), the essence of what it looks and feels like to bring God into one's life (*The Holy Experience*), the common encounter with unexpected and unwanted change (*When Everything Changes, Change Everything*), the ways now open to humanity to manage its seismic political, economic, and social upheaval (*The Storm Before the Calm*), and the one thing in all of this that has true significance in our lives, based on the single desire of the human soul (*The Only Thing That Matters*).

The powerful treatise on how to fully and powerfully utilize the metaphysics of the universe fills the pages of

Happier Than God, CWG's formula for creating right liveli-hood is the topic of *Bringers of the Light*, and a pinpoint sum-mary of the core concepts in the original 3,000 pages of dialogue can be found in *What God Said*, in which those concepts are reduced to 1,000 words, with chapters fol-lowing that explain each concept in detail. A concise state-ment serving anyone who may be wondering what all of the CWG books are about, but may not have time to delve into this whole body of work, is contained in the small volume *What God Wants*. Then, a highly focused exploration of the most damaging misunderstandings of Deity that bil-lions of humans have held for thousands of years is offered in *God's Message to the World: You've Got Me All Wrong*.

Concluding the list of supplementary texts: Wonder-fully useful strategies for bringing the major messages of CWG to humanity's offspring, from post-toddler to pre-adolescent years, is presented in *Conversations with God for Parents: Sharing the Messages with Children*, co-authored with Laurie Farley and Emily Filmore. A look at the intersec-tion of CWG and traditional healing professions is found in *Where God and Medicine Meet*, co-authored with Brit Cooper, M.D., and finally, a teacher's guide for persons wishing to offer classes in this material has been published under the title *The Conversations with God Companion*.

Here is the Complete Title List of All CWG Books:

DIALOGUE BOOKS:

Conversations with God, Book 1

Conversations with God, Book 2

Conversations with God, Book 3

Friendship with God

Communion with God

The New Revelations

Tomorrow's God

Home with God

Conversations with God, Book 4: Awaken the Species

SUPPLEMENTARY TITLES:

1. *What God Wants*
2. *Bringers of the Light*
3. *Recreating Your Self*
4. *Questions and Answers on Conversations with God*
5. *Conversations with God for Teens*
6. *Moments of Grace*
7. *Neale Donald Walsch on Relationships*
8. *Neale Donald Walsch on Holistic Living*
9. *Neale Donald Walsch on Abundance and Right Livelihood*
10. *Happier Than God*
11. *The Holy Experience*

ADDITIONAL TEXTS:

A LOOK AT THE MATERIAL
IN THIS BOOK SERIES:
Below is a 50-Question Exploration of the major points placed before humanity in the *Conversations with God* texts. This may be used as a Test with Answer Key for CWG

teachers and students. It may also be beneficial to review the questions and answers here to get a begin sense of the breadth and scope of the topics covered this body of work—and perhaps inspire you.

Question #1:
What are the Three Statements of Ultimate Truth from Book 1 of *Conversations with God*?

Answer #1:

1. We are all one.

2. There is enough.

3. There is nothing that you have to do.

Text References in support of this answer:
(1) We are all one. *CWG, Book 1*, p. 36
(2) There is enough. *CWG, Book 1*, p. 165; *CWG Companion*, p. 151
(3) There is nothing you have to do. *CWG, Book 1*, p. 145; *Book 3*, p. 14

Question #2:
Please explain the Be-Do-Have Paradigm.

Answer #2:
Most people believe that if I DO this, then I'll HAVE that, then I'll BE happy. CWG tells us that most people have the flow of life backward. The dialogue invites us to come from a state of BE-ingness first. Then what we DO and HAVE will spring from that place, thus more joyfully creating our experience.

...port of this answer:
...71/*Book 3*, pp. 14, 15/*CWG*
...2

....

...ttitudes of Godliness?

...yful, Loving, Accepting, Blessing, and

...nces in support of this answer:
...1, pp. 65, 66

....

...estion #4:
...lease State the Law of Opposites and how it works.

Answer #4:
"In the absence of that which you are *not*, that which you *are* is not." In the Realm of the Physical (also known as the Realm of the Relative) nothing exists without its opposite. The moment you declare yourself to be anything, everything unlike it will come into your experience. This allows you to know yourself as what you've declared yourself to be. You cannot know "hot" until you experience cold. You cannot know "fast" unless you experience "slow." You cannot know yourself as "tall" if there is no one and nothing "short" to compare yourself to, etc.

Text Reference in support of this answer:
CWG, Book 1, p. 27

....

Question #5:
What is a "Divine Dichotomy"?

Answer #5:
It is when two apparently contradictory truths co-exist simultaneously in the same space. Instead of such a circumstance presenting a choice of *either* this *or* that, it offers the possibility of *both* this *and* that. "Either/Or" is replaced by "Both/And."

Text References in support of this answer:
CWG, Book 1, pp. 126, 133,186

....

Question #6:
What are the Ten Commitments?

Answer #6:
God has given us a Commitment to provide us with "sure and certain signs" that we are on the path to our experience of God. There are certain things that you shall do *spontaneously* and *automatically.* That is how you will *know* you are on The Path! Specifically, God said: You will know that you are on the Path to God because I will give you these signs: When you are on the Path to God . . .

  1. You shall love God with all your heart, all your mind and all your soul.

2. You shall not use God's name in vain, nor call upon God for frivolous things.

3. You shall keep a day for God, to re-connect with your Divine Self, so you don't stay too long in your illusion.

4. You shall honor your mother and father, as well as your Mother/Father God. Thus, you shall honor everyone.

5. You shall not willfully kill without cause. This includes all life forms, not just humans.

6. You shall not defile the purity of love with dishonesty or deceit, as this would be adulterous.

7. You shall not steal or cheat, or connive to harm another.

8. You shall not lie.

9. You shall not covet your neighbor's spouse, because you will know that all others are your spouse.

10. You shall not covet your neighbor's goods, because you shall know that all goods can be yours, and that all of your goods belong to the world.

Text References in support of this answer:
CWG, Book 1, pp. 96, 97

Question #7:

What are the Triune Truths?

Answer #7:

The Triune Truth is that all of life is a Trinity, or Triune, Reality. That is, there is a "three-in-one" quality to every aspect of life. In some religions this 3-in-1 characteristic is referred to as "Father, Son, and Holy Spirit." Other places where we find this 3-in-1 aspect demonstrating itself:

We say that a thing is Physical, Nonphysical, or Metaphysical; we talk of Knowing, Experiencing, and Being; we speak of the Superconscious, Conscious, Subconscious; we use the phrase Body, Mind, and Spirit; we describe our universe as made up of Energy, Matter, or Anti-matter; we describe human activity as being expressed in Thought, Word, and Deed; we refer to the times of our life as Past, Present, and Future; as well, we speak of Before, Now, and After; when considering the element of place or space, we talk in terms of Here, There, or Between.

Text References in support of this answer:

CWG, Book 1, pp. 23, 30, 31, 73

....

Question #8:

Name the Three Laws of Reality.

Answer #8:

1. Thought is creative—and collective thought creates collectively

2. Fear attracts like energy—what you fear, you attract

3. Love is all there is.

Text References in support of this answer:
CWG, Book 1, pp. 54, 56

....

Question #9:
Name the Three Functions of Life.

Answer #9:

1. The function of the soul is to indicate its desires (not impose them).

2. The function of the mind is to choose from its alternatives.

3. The function of the body is to act out that choice.

Text References in support of this answer:
CWG, Book 1, p. 196

....

Question #10:
CWG gives us Six Signs of a Decision to Live Consciously. What are they?

Answer #10:

1. Not long ago all we wanted to do was to stay here (in the Realm of the Physical). Now

all we want to do is leave (to get back to the
Realm of the Spiritual). We thought our Basic
Instinct was Survival. Now we know that our
Basic Instinct is the Expression of Divinity.

2. Not long ago we killed things. Now we can't
kill anything without knowing exactly what
we're doing, and why.

3. Not long ago we lived life as though it had
no purpose. Now we know it has no purpose
save the one we give it.

4. Not long ago we begged God to bring us
truth. Now we tell God our truth.

5. Not long ago we sought to be rich and
famous. Now we seek simply to be our wonderful selves.

6. Not long ago we feared God. Now we love
God enough to call It our equal.

Text References in support of this answer:
CWG, Book 1, pp. 156, 157

....

Question #11:
Please explain "What you resist persists."

Answer #11:
When you resist something, you give it energy, which
continues to create it in your reality. If something is not
to your liking, instead of resisting, look right at it until

it ceases to have its illusory form. That is, look at it until you see right through the illusion to Ultimate Reality.

Text References in support of this answer:
CWG, Book 1, pp. 102, 103

....

Question #12:
What is the purpose of the soul?

Answer #12:
To turn its grandest concept of Itself into its greatest experience.

Text References in support of this answer:
CWG, Book 1, p. 22

....

Question #13:
Name the Two Sponsoring Thoughts upon which all other Thoughts are based.

Answer #13:
Love and Fear.

Text References in support of this answer:
CWG, Book 1, p. 15

....

Question #14:
Explain the difference between pain and suffering.

Answer #14:

Pain is a physical or mental feeling, caused by a stimulus of some kind. Suffering is your decision about it. Suffering arises out of a decision that something that is happening is not supposed to be happening or should not be occurring. Suffering ends when the person makes a conscious decision to hold a specific pain in a new way. In the case of either physical or emotional pain, one may reduce or disappear suffering by deciding to love what is happening, knowing that it will ultimately prove to be for the highest good. We thus remove the "woe is me" aspect (as in a woman giving birth, or a person having a tooth extracted).

Text References in support of this answer:
CWG, Book 1, pp. 105, 107

Question #15:
Complete the following sentence: Relationships work best when you . . .

Answer #15:
. . . do what's best for you.

Text References in support of this answer:
CWG, Book 1, pp. 130–132/*CWG Companion*, p. 121

Question #16:
Complete the following sentence: Life proceeds out of . . .

Answer #16:
. . . your intentions for it.

Text References in support of this answer:
CWG, Book 1, pp. 118

....

Question #17:
Complete the following sentence: All true benefits are . . .

Answer #17:
. . . mutual.

Text References in support of this answer:
Friendship with God, p. 336 (Elisabeth Kübler-Ross)/*CWG Companion*, p. 118

....

Question #18:
Complete the following sentence: Every act is an act of . . .

Answer #18:
. . . self-definition.

Text References in support of this answer:
When Everything Changes, Change Everything, p. 267/*CWG Companion*, p. 173

....

Question #19:
God says you may not have anything you want. Why is this so?

Answer #19:

Because the mere act of wanting something tells the Universe that you don't have it, and the Universe has no choice but to reflect that back in your reality. You end up getting more "wanting what you want," because God always says "yes" to your Sponsoring Thought.

Text References in support of this answer:
CWG, Book 1, p. 11

....

Question #20:
What are the Five Levels of Truth Telling?

Answer #20:

1. Tell the truth to yourself about yourself.

2. Tell the truth to yourself about another.

3. Tell your truth to another about yourself.

4. Tell the truth to another about that other.

5. Tell the truth to everyone about everything.

Text References in support of this answer:
CWG, Book 2, p. 3, 4

....

Question #21:
What are the Three Core Concepts of Holistic Living?

Answer #21:

1. Awareness

2. Honesty

3. Responsibility

Text References in support of this answer:
CWG, Book 3, p. 334 (also referred to as The Triangular Code)

....

Question #22:
Name the Three Tools of Creation.

Answer #22:

1. Thought

2. Word

3. Deed (Action)

Text References in support of this answer:
CWG, Book 1, p. 91/*Friendship with God*, p. 254

....

Question #23:
List the Seven Steps to *Friendship with God*.

Answer #23:

1. Know God

2. Trust God

3. Love God

4. Embrace God

5. Use God

6. Help God

7. Thank God

Text References in support of this answer:
Friendship with God, p. 57

....

Question #24:
CWG says there are Three Basic Life Principles. The first is Functionality. Name the others.

Answer #24:

1. Functionality

2. Adaptability

3. Sustainability

Text References in support of this answer:
The New Revelations, p. 223/*When Everything Changes, Change Everything*, p. 167

....

Question #25:
What is the 15-word New Gospel?

Answer #25:
We are all one. Ours is not a better way, ours is merely another way.

Text References in support of this answer:
Friendship with God, pp. 153, 381, 425

Question #26:

The Two Magic Questions are: Is this Who I Am? And . . .

Answer #26:

What would love do now?

Text References in support of this answer:

CWG, Book 1, p. 130

....

Question #27:

Name the Four Levels of Consciousness

Answer #27:

1. Subconscious

2. Conscious

3. Superconscious

4. Supraconscious

Text References in support of this answer:

Friendship with God, pp. 115-117

....

Question #28:

There are six Levels of Knowing. Name at least three.

Answer #28:

1. There are those who do not know, and don't know that they don't know. They are children. Nurture them.

2. There are those who do not know and know that they don't know. They are willing. Teach them.

3. There are those who do not know, but think that they know. They are dangerous. Avoid them.

4. There are those who know, but don't know that they know. They are asleep. Wake them.

5. There are those who know, but pretend that they don't know. They are actors. Enjoy them. But do not get caught up in their dramas.

6. There are those who know, and who know that they know. Do not follow them, because if they *know* that they know, they would not *have* you follow them. Yet listen very carefully to what they have to say, for they may *remind* you of what *you* already know. That may be the very reason you have called them to you.

Text References in support of this answer:
Friendship with God, p. 289

....

Question #29:

What are the Three Levels of Awareness? (Clue: the first is "Hope.")

Answer #29:

1. Hope

2. Faith (Belief)

3. Knowing

Hope is the first level of awareness. It is far better than the feeling of "no hope," but it is an elementary level of awareness, because it suggests that a positive outcome in any given situation is a possibility, but not a guarantee. So, one is said to have "hope."

Faith is the second level of awareness. It is greater in energy than "hope" because it suggests that while negative outcomes are possible, a positive outcome is assured in this particular case. So, one is said to have "faith."

Knowing is the highest level of awareness. It is greater than either "hope" or "faith" because it declares that no negative outcome is possible under any circumstances, but that all outcomes are positive, and therefore welcome and not resisted, since all move us forward on our evolutionary path, and lead us back Home. We are thus said to be in a place of "knowing" that nothing "bad" can happen to us, ever. This is true, of course, given who and what we are.

Text References in support of this answer:
Friendship with God, p. 107

....

Question #30:
List the Ten Illusions of Humans.

Answer #30:

    1. Need exists.

    2. Failure exists.

3. Disunity exists.

4. Insufficiency exists.

5. Requirement exists.

6. Judgment exists.

7. Condemnation exists.

8. Conditionality exists.

9. Superiority exists.

10. Ignorance exists.

Text References in support of this answer:
Communion with God, pp. 15, 16
Happier Than God, pp. 251, 252

....

Question #31:
What is the Cultural Story that Humanity has created
from these illusions? (Hint: It has 10 points)

Answer #31:
Because of the ten illusions we have come to falsely
believe that . . .

1. God has an agenda. (Need exists)

2. The outcome of life is in doubt. (Failure
   exists)

3. We are separate from God. (Disunity exists)

4. There is not enough. (Insufficiency exists)

5. There is something we have to do. (Requirement exists)

6. If we don't do it we will be punished. (Judgment exists)

7. That punishment is everlasting damnation. (Condemnation exists)

8. Love is, therefore, conditional. (Conditionality exists)

9. Knowing and meeting the conditions makes us superior. (Superiority exists)

10. We do not know that these are illusions. (Ignorance exists)

Text References in support of this answer:
Communion with God, p. 18
Happier Than God , pp. 252, 253

Question #32:
What is the Triad Process?

Answer #32:
The Triad Process is a way to use the illusions to experience ourselves totally differently in any given situation when we are confronted with an illusion in life.
The process is . . .

1. See the illusion for what it is.

2. Decide what it means.

3. Re-create ourselves anew.

Text References in support of this answer:
Communion with God, p. 181

....

Question #33:
Complete the following sentence: In the absence of that which you are not. . .

Answer #33:
. . . that which you are, is not.

Text References in support of this answer:
CWG, Book 3, pp. 205, 348, 353/The *CWG Companion*, p. 31/*When Everything Changes, Change Everything* , p. 193

....

Question #34:
Name the Five Fallacies About God and the Five Fallacies About Life.

Answer #34:
The Five Fallacies About God...

1. People believe that God needs something.

2. People believe that it's possible for God to not get what He needs.

3. People believe God has separated Himself from them because they have failed to give Him what He needs.

4. People believe that God needs something so much He requires them to give it to Him from their separated position.

5. People believe that God will destroy them if they don't give Him what He needs.

Text References in support of this answer:
The New Revelations, pp. 29, 30/*Tomorrow's God*, p. 111

The Five Fallacies About Life...

1. People are separate from each other.

2. There is not enough of what people need to be happy.

3. People think they must compete for what they think there is not enough of.

4. Some people are better than other people.

5. It is okay for people to kill each other to resolve the differences created by all the other fallacies.

Text References in support of this answer: *The New Revelations*, pp. 37, 38/*Tomorrow's God*, p. 111, 112

....

Question #35:
Name at least 5 of the 9 New Revelations from the book *The New Revelations*.

Answer #35:

1. God has always communicated with human beings, and still does so today.

2. Every human being is as special as every other who has ever lived, lives now, or ever will live.

We are all messengers about life, to life, in every moment.

3. No path to God is better than any other path. There is no "one true religion" and no group of people who are the "chosen ones."

4. God needs nothing and has no requirements of anyone. God is pure joy in and of Itself.

5. God is not a singular super being outside of us, and has none of the emotional "needs" of humans. God cannot be hurt or damaged in any way, and therefore has no need to punish humans.

6. There is only One Thing, and all things are part of the One Thing There Is.

7. There is no such thing as Right and Wrong. There is only What Works and What Does Not Work, given what you are seeking to be, do, or have.

8. You are not your body. Your body is something you *have*, not something you are. Like God, you are without limits and without end.

9. You cannot die, and you will never be condemned to eternal damnation.

Text References in support of this answer: *The New Revelations*, pp. 339-341

....

Question #36:
Write out the Five Steps to Peace.

Answer #36:

1. Acknowledge that some of our old beliefs about God and Life are no longer working.

2. Acknowledge that there may be something we don't understand about God and Life, the understanding of which would change everything.

3. Be willing for a new understanding about God and Life to come forth, and allow this understanding to produce a new way of life on Earth.

4. Be courageous enough to explore and examine this new understanding and if it aligns with our inner knowing, enlarge our belief system to include it.

5. Live our lives as demonstrations of our highest beliefs, rather than denials of them.

Text References in support of this answer:
The New Revelations, p. 14

....

Question #37:
Name at least 5 of the 9 characteristics of *Tomorrow's God*.

Answer #37:

1. *Tomorrow's God* doesn't require anyone to believe in God. p. 22

2. *Tomorrow's God* has no gender, size, shape, color, or any characteristic of an individual living being. p. 23

3. *Tomorrow's God* talks with everyone, all the time. p. 140

4. *Tomorrow's God* is separate from nothing and is Everything Everywhere. p. 32

5. *Tomorrow's God* is not a singular super being, but rather, the extraordinary process of life Itself, p. 71

6. *Tomorrow's God* is always changing. p. 76

7. *Tomorrow's God* has no needs. p. 169

8. *Tomorrow's God* does not ask to be served; rather, It is the servant of all of life. p. 180

9. *Tomorrow's God* is unconditionally loving. p. 196

Text References in support of this answer:
Tomorrow's God, p. 386 (the list; individual explanations on the pages noted above)

....

Question #38:
Name at least 10 of the 18 Remembrances.

Answer #38:

1. Dying is something you do for you, p. 7

2. You are always the cause of your own death, no matter where or how you die. p. 8

3. You cannot die against your will. p. 10

4. No path back Home is better than any other path. p. 23

5. Death is never a tragedy. Rather, it is always a gift. p. 42

6. You and God are one and there is no separation between you. p. 70

7. Death does not exist. p. 89

8. You can't change Ultimate Reality, but you can change your experience of it. p. 91

9. The reason for all of life is the desire of God to know Itself in its own experience. p. 153

10. Life is eternal. p. 166

11. The timing and circumstances of death are always perfect. p. 171

12. The death of every person always serves the agenda of every other person who is aware of it. Indeed, that is *why* that person is aware of it. Therefore, no life or death is ever in vain. p. 181

13. Birth and death are the same thing. p. 202

14. You are constantly creating, both in life and in death. p. 217

15. Evolution never ends. p. 254

16. Death is reversible. p. 256

17. When you die you'll be greeted by all your loved ones—those who have passed before you, and those who will pass after you. p. 299

18. Free choice is the act of pure creation, God's signature, and your gift, glory, and power, always. p. 311

Text References in support of this answer:
Home with God, pp. 325-326 (the list; individual explanations on the pages noted above)

....

Question #39:
Happier Than God tells us that Life expresses itself in essentially five ways. What are they?

Answer #39:

1. The Energy of Attraction, which gives us power.

2. The Law of Opposites, which gives us opportunity.

3. The Gift of Wisdom, which gives us discernment.

4. The Joy of Wonder, which gives us imagination.

5. The Presence of Cycles, which gives us eternity.

Text References in support of this answer:
Happier Than God, pp. 54, 55

....

Question #40:
What are the Four Fundamental Questions in Life?

Answer #40:

1. Who am I?

2. Where am I?

3. Why am I where I am?

4. What am I doing here?

Text References in support of this answer:
When Everything Changes, Change Everything, asked on pp. 185, 190 and answered on pp. 190-199; also in *The Storm Before the Calm* as four of the Seven Simple Questions. The other three:

(1) How is it possible for 7 billion members of what purports to be a highly evolved species to all want the same thing—survival, safety, security, peace, prosperity, opportunity, happiness, and love—and for them to be utterly unable to produce it, *even after thousands of years of trying?*
(2) Is it possible that there is something we don't fully understand about God and about Life, the understanding of which would change everything?

(3) Is it possible that there is something we don't fully understand about *ourselves* and who we are, the understanding of which would change our lives for the better forever?

....

Question #41:
Name at least 10 of the 17 Steps to Being Happier Than God

Answer #41:

1. Bring an end to separation theology. p. 206

2. Stay in touch with Who I Am. p. 209

3. Give others every experience I seek. p. 210

4. Be clear that nothing I see is real. p. 212

5. Decide that I am not my "story." p. 213

6. Have only preferences. p. 216

7. See the perfection in everything. p. 220

8. Skip the drama. p. 221

9. Understand sadness. p. 223

10. Stop arguing with life. p. 225

11. Drop all expectations. p. 227

12. Have compassion for myself. p. 228

13. Speak my truth as soon as I know it. p. 229

14. Watch the energies; catch the vibe. p. 231

15. Smile. p. 223

16. Sing. p. 234

17. Know what to do when things are really "bad." p. 235

Text References in support of this answer:
Happier Than God, pp. 206-235 (the list; individual explanations on the pages noted above)

Question #42:

List the Nine Changes That Can Change Everything

Answer #42:

1. Change my decision to "go it alone." p. 29

2. Change my choice of emotions. p. 57

3. Change my choice of thoughts. p. 65

4. Change my choice of truths. p. 70

5. Change my idea about change itself. p. 161

6. Change my idea about why change occurs. p. 173

7. Change my idea about future change. p. 218

8. Change my idea about life. p. 238

9. Change my identity. p. 272

Text References in support of this answer:

When Everything Changes, Change Everything, p. 7 (the list; individual explanations on the pages noted above)

....

Question #43:

Throughout life we experience Reality in one of three ways. Name the Three Realities.

Answer #43:

1. The Distorted reality

2. The Observed reality

3. The Ultimate reality

Text References in support of this answer:
When Everything Changes, Change Everything, pp. 66, 131, 132 ("The Triune Reality")

....

Question #44:
What are the three kinds of Truth that the Mind produces?

Answer #44:

    1. The Imagined truth

    2. The Apparent truth

    3. The Actual truth

Text References in support of this answer:
When Everything Changes, Change Everything, pp. 71, 131, 132

....

Question #45:
In the Mechanics of the Mind, what is the Line of Causality?

Answer #45:
Event + Data + Truth + Thought + Emotion + Experience = Reality

Text References in support of this answer: *When Everything Changes, Change Everything*, p. 70

....

Question #46:

What four additional elements are added to the Line of Causality under the System of the Soul?

Answer #46:

Perspective + Perception + Belief + Behavior = Experience

Text References in support of this answer:

When Everything Changes, Change Everything, p. 208

....

Question #47:

Why does change occur in your life?

Answer #47:

All change occurs because we want it to, in order to produce personal growth and evolution of the soul. Life is a process, and that process is called Change. (Change is an announcement of Life's intention to go on. Change is the fundamental impulse of Life Itself.)

Text References in support of this answer:

When Everything Changes, Change Everything, p. 168

....

Question #48:

Complete the following sentence: All change is.

Answer #48:

. . . for the better. (There is no such thing as change for the worse.)

Text References in support of this answer:

When Everything Changes, Change Everything, p. 158

Question #49:

What are the Three Realms in the Kingdom of God?

Answer #49:

1. The Realm of the Spiritual (also called the Realm of the Absolute, and the Realm of Knowing)

2. The Realm of the Physical (also called the Realm of the Relative, and the Realm of Experience)

3. The Realm of the Spirisical (the combination of the Realm of the Spiritual & Physical; also called the Realm of Pure Being)

Text References in support of this answer:

When Everything Changes, Change Everything, pp. 191, 192, 195, 196

....

Question #50:

What is the most important single message of *Conversations with God*?

Answer #50:

We are all One. (Also often asked: "What is God's Message to the World" Answer in five words: "You've got me all wrong.")

Text References in support of this answer:

Book 1 (and Neale on the *Today Show* on NBC with Matt Lauer)

About the Author

NEALE DONALD WALSCH is a modern day spiritual messenger whose work has touched the lives of millions. He has written twenty-nine books on contemporary spirituality in the twenty years since he reported having an experience in which he felt the presence of The Divine, began writing questions to God on a yellow legal pad, and received answers in a process that he describes as exactly like taking dictation. What emerged from that encounter was the nine-part *Conversations with God* series, which has been published in every major language of the world.

Mr. Walsch has told his readers and the media—which has brought global attention to his experience—that everyone is having conversations with God all the time, and that the question is not: To whom does God talk? The question is: Who listens?

He says his whole life has been changed as a result of his own decision to listen. He took notes on the questions in his heart and the answers he was receiving, so that he would always remember his exchanges with Deity. It wasn't until later that he realized he was being invited to place these words into the world, as one of many throughout history who have made their very best effort to hear and to articulate God's messages. He knows that everyone is receiving these messages, and invites all people everywhere to both share them and live them as best they can, for Neale believes the world would change overnight if only a fraction of its people embraced God's most important message of all: *You've got me all wrong.*

Related Titles from Rainbow Ridge

Read more about them at *www.rainbowridgebooks.com*.

God's Message to the World: You've Got Me All Wrong
by Neale Donald Walsch

Conversations with God for Parents
by Neale Donald Walsch,
Laura Lankins Farley, and Emily A. Filmore

*Consciousness: Bridging the Gap between Conventional Science
and the New Super Science of Quantum Mechanics*
by Eva Herr

*Dying to Know You:
Proof of God in the Near-Death Experience*
by P. M. H. Atwater

Rita's World: Explanations from the Other Side
by Frank DeMarco

Messiah's Handbook: Reminders for the Advanced Soul
by Richard Bach

When the Horses Whisper
by Rosalyn Berne

Quantum Economics
by Amit Goswami

Soul Courage
by Tara-jenelle Walsch

The Cosmic Internet
by Frank DeMarco

God Within
by Patti Conklin

Liquid Luck:
The Good Fortune Handbook
by Joe Gallenberger

Imagine Yourself Well
by Frank DeMarco

What to Do When You're Dead
by Sondra Sneed

The Healing Curve
by Sara Chetkin

....

Rainbow Ridge Books publishes spiritual, metaphysical,
and self-help titles, and is distributed by Square
One Publishers in Garden City Park, New York.

To contact authors and editors, peruse our titles,
and see submission guidelines, please visit
our website at *www.rainbowridgebooks.com*.

For orders and catalogs, please call toll-free: (877) 900-BOOK.